FREDDIE THE FROG® BEYOND THE BOOKS

TEACHING TIPS, TOOLS AND ASSESSMENT
BY SHARON BURCH

SHAWNEE PRESS
EXCLUSIVELY DISTRIBUTED BY
HAL•LEONARD®
7777 W. BLUEMOUND RD. P.O. BOX 13819 MILWAUKEE, WI 53213

Copyright © 2011 by HAL LEONARD CORPORATION
International Copyright Secured   All Rights Reserved

Visit Hal Leonard Online at
www.halleonard.com

Visit Shawnee Press Online at
www.shawneepress.com

Contact Us:
Hal Leonard
7777 West Bluemound Road
Milwaukee, WI 53213
Email: info@halleonard.com

In Europe contact:
Hal Leonard Europe Limited
Distribution Centre, Newmarket Road
Bury St Edmunds, Suffolk, IP33 3YB
Email: info@halleonardeurope.com

In Australia contact:
Hal Leonard Australia Pty. Ltd.
4 Lentara Court
Cheltenham, Victoria, 3192 Australia
Email: info@halleonard.com.au

DIGITAL DOWNLOAD CODE
To access DIGITAL CONTENT, go to:
www.halleonard.com/mylibrary

Enter Code
6188-3803-9008-5925

This publication is intended for use by one school or organization only. The original purchaser of this book has permission to reproduce and distribute print copies of the assessment material on pages 35-42, 45-46, 51-52, and may project or reproduce the digital content for educational use only. No other part of this publication may be reproduced or distributed in any form or by any means without the prior written permission of the Publisher.

TABLE OF CONTENTS

LESSON 1: INTRODUCTION TO FREDDIE THE FROG® PUPPET — 6
Introduction to the FREDDIE THE FROG® Puppet
"Hello, Freddie" song
Teaching with a frog

LESSON 2: INTRODUCING TREBLE CLEF NOTES — 8
Freddie the Frog® and the Thump in the Night (Book/CD)
Setting up the story
Review using the pages at the end of the book
"Froggie Went A'Courtin'"
"Eli's Hokey Pokey"

LESSON 3: DISCOVERING FREDDIE'S ABC'S (THE MUSIC ALPHABET) — 9
A captivating cue set: The magic of a puppet
Freddie's Name That Tune Game
Review using *Thump in the Night* Flashcards
Music stories on barred instruments

LESSON 4: INTRODUCING RHYTHM, BEAT AND TEMPO — 11
Freddie the Frog® and the Mysterious Wahooooo (Book/CD)
Setting up the story with mini-maracas and rhythm sticks
Review using the Tempo Island Magnetic Rhythm Board set

LESSON 5: COMPOSING 4-BEAT RHYTHM PATTERNS — 13
The Tempo Game!
Craft Sticks

LESSON 6: THE 12-BAR BLUES CHORD PROGRESSION — 16
Create Rhythm Patterns to the 12-Bar Blues
Add Boomwhackers

LESSON 7: CALL AND RESPONSE ON PITCHED INSTRUMENTS — 18
4-Count Melodic Improvisation
Call and Response

LESSON 8: INTRODUCING BASS CLEF NOTES — 20
Freddie the Frog® and the Bass Clef Monster (Book/CD)
Freddie's ABCs – forwards and backwards!
"Hop 'N Flop Shuffle"

LESSON 9: INTRODUCTION TO SOLFEGE (DO, RE, MI) AND CLEF SIGNS — 23
Freddie's Mystery Singing Game and introduction to Solfege using "The Closet Key"
Identifying the difference between the treble clef and bass clef signs
Review using *Bass Clef Monster* and *Thump in the Night* flashcards

LESSON 10: INTRODUCING MORE TREBLE CLEF NOTES — 25
Freddie the Frog® and the Secret of Crater Island (Book/CD)
Review using *Secret of Crater Island* Flashcards
Discovering the stories on the grand staff

LESSON 11: COMPOSING A 12-BAR BLUES SONG — 27
Simple blues song composition
Review note names using all of the flashcards

LESSON 12: MATCHING GAME WITH NOTE NAME FLASHCARDS — 28

LESSON 13: INDEPENDENT PRACTICE STUDENT FLASHCARDS — 29
Photocopy reproducible student flashcards, cut and stack
Plastic Ziploc sandwich bags
Double Rotating Circle

LESSON 14: INTERNET GAME REVIEW AND COLORING PAGES — 30
www.FreddieTheFrog.com
Coloring Pages
Parent Note

ASSESSMENT TOOLS AND IDEAS — 31

INTERACTIVE ONLINE GAMES AND COLORING PAGES — 33

INTERACTIVE WHITEBOARD LESSONS — 34
Freddie's Mystery Song ("Closet Key")
Freddie's Mystery Song ("Engine, Engine")
4-Beat to 12-Bar Fun

APPENDIX A: REPRODUCIBLE ASSESSMENT TOOLS — 35
Assessment Report Sheet Samples
Assessment Report Sheet Forms for K-2 and Grades 3-6
Grade level expectations rubric for parents
Assessment Spreadsheet for recording student assessments
Parent Note

APPENDIX B: REPRODUCIBLE STUDENT FLASHCARDS — 43
Flashcard Instructions, Treble Clef Notes, Bass Clef Notes, Rhythm Notation, Vocabulary Terms

APPENDIX C: REPRODUCIBLE COLORING PAGES — 47
Freddie the Frog® and the Thump in the Night
Freddie the Frog® and the Secret of Crater Island
Freddie the Frog® and the Bass Clef Monster
Freddie the Frog® and the Mysterious Wahooooo

APPENDIX D: WHAT'S AVAILABLE VIA DIGITAL ACCESS? — 53
Freddie the Frog® and the Mysterious Wahooooo Stick Rhythms
Tempo Island Rhythm Background
5 Characters: Freddie the Frog, Eli the Elephant, Purple Elephant, Bobaloo Baboon and Orangutan-tang
Interactive Whiteboard Lessons
Reproducible Student Flashcards
25 Coloring Pages
Assessment Spreadsheet and Templates

INTRODUCTION

FREDDIE THE FROG® – HOW IT ALL BEGAN

I created the first Freddie the Frog® story as a storyteller with an oversized staff mat and a frog puppet on my hand. A group of pre-school age kids sat around the mat eagerly awaiting a good story. I can be pretty dramatic and love to tell a good story. I hoped the students would be pulled into the story and visualize the characters and events of the story when looking at specific places on the staff mat, similar to looking at a map. It would serve as an introduction to reading treble clef note names. The characters and events began with the corresponding letter of the music note on that line or space. I was pleasantly surprised when they not only connected the key elements to the places on the staff, but they had fallen in love with the frog puppet on my hand. They remembered the events and characters of the story when I pointed to the places on the staff and they wanted to talk to Freddie! He was real! They asked if they could give him a hug. Thinking quickly, I responded that of course they could, if they could line up quietly at the door. As quiet as mice, the preschool children tiptoed to the door so they could give my frog puppet a hug!

At the next music class, the students entered asking for Freddie. Once again, I got Freddie on my hand and pretended that I could hear him talking to me, asking if we could play a game. I related what Freddie had "said" to me, and then told Freddie that we could play his game if the kids did a great job listening and doing their job. The kids nodded their heads in agreement. That was the beginning.

Freddie comes to every music class and the kids eagerly wait to see what Freddie wants to do that day. Many days we just sing his *Hello Song* to begin class and then he sits and "watches" us for the rest of class until it is time to leave. Freddie loves hugs, so on my hand he goes and we stand at the door awaiting hugs. Of course, you can only give Freddie a hug if you are "doing your job" in line.

I had used puppets in my room before, but sporadically--only using a puppet that was specific to a certain song or poem. Combining a story with a puppet gives the puppet a personality and makes him a friend to the kids. Having the same puppet come to each music class strengthens the relationship and creates consistency. The kids fall in love with music class because they have fallen in love with Freddie the Frog®.

When the students meet Freddie as a preschooler or kindergarten student, they look forward to seeing him all the way through second grade, and sometimes third grade. The rest of **Beyond the Books** contains tips, tools and tricks that work for me in my classroom, using Freddie the Frog® and his first four adventure stories as a foundation to introduce and build upon.

Enjoy!
Sharon Burch
K-3 Music Teacher and Creator/Author of Freddie the Frog® Books

FREDDIE THE FROG® BOOKS AND MATERIALS REFERRED TO IN THIS RESOURCE BOOK

See pages 55 & 56 for more details.

- FREDDIE THE FROG® Teacher's Puppet

- *Freddie the Frog® and the Thump in the Night* book/audio CD
- *Thump in the Night* Flashcard Set

- *Freddie the Frog® and the Mysterious Wahooooo* book/audio CD
- *Tempo Island* Magnetic Rhythm Board Set

- *Freddie the Frog® and the Bass Clef Monster* book/audio CD
- *Bass Clef Monster* Flashcard Set
- *Bass Clef Monster* Poster

- *Freddie the Frog® and the Secret of Crater Island* book/audio CD
- *Secret of Crater Island* Flashcard Set
- *Treble Clef Island* Poster

WEBSITES

Games and Coloring Pages
www.FreddieTheFrog.com

VIDEO CLIPS, AUDIO CLIPS AND OTHER TEACHING TOOLS

www.K3MusicTeachers.com

Sharon Burch began teaching general music in 1987. Constantly pursuing the best methods of educationally connecting with students, she is a National Board Certified Teacher in Early and Middle Childhood Music, a certified teacher with the International Piano Teaching Foundation, holds a master's degree as a Professional Educator and uses a combination of strategies to enable kids to experience concepts in the classroom. Teaching creatively, Sharon introduced Freddie the Frog® to her classroom of music students in 1995 and discovered the magic of games, storytelling and puppetry in teaching. She authored *Freddie the Frog® and the Thump in the Night, Freddie the Frog® and the Bass Clef Monster, Freddie the Frog® and the Mysterious Wahooooo,* and *Freddie the Frog® and the Secret of Crater Island* as the first of several adventuresome stories introducing fundamental music concepts. *Freddie the Frog® and the Flying Jazz Kitten* introduces jazz through scat and improvisation. Sharon serves on the national Jazz Education Network Elementary Jazz Committee and enjoys sharing her teaching strategies at music conferences and clinics with teachers around the globe. Sharon teaches general music to the K-3 students in the Centerville Community School District in Centerville, Iowa.

Lesson 1

INTRODUCTION TO FREDDIE THE FROG® PUPPET
- Introduction to the Freddie the Frog® Puppet
- "Hello, Freddie" song
- Teaching with a frog

INTRODUCTION TO THE FREDDIE THE FROG® PUPPET

On the first day of school, the kids coming to you for the first time in music are a little shy. The students will be worried about this new situation, new room, and new teacher. But as soon as they see Freddie, their fears go away, and their whole focus is on this little stuffed frog on your hand.

Now that their attention is on this little stuffed frog that actually moves and talks, they are curious. Freddie becomes worried, and hides behind the teacher's back. Now you have all of the students' attention. I pretend that I can hear Freddie. I ask him what is wrong. He shakes his head and says he is scared. He is afraid that the students do not like him. That's when I turn to the students and ask if it is true. Of course, the kids shake their heads and say no. But Freddie refuses to come from behind my back. So I turn to the students once again, and ask if they would like to learn Freddie's hello song. I tell them he would probably not be scared if they learned his song and sang it for him. If you work with preschool or kindergarten, then you know what their response will be. They immediately are singing, not thinking about themselves at all. The song I teach them is "Hello, Freddie."

"HELLO, FREDDIE"

(sung to the tune of "Where is Thumbkin?")

Hello, Freddie.
Hello, Freddie.
Who are you?
Who are you?
We are friends of Freddie.
We are friends of Freddie.
How are you? (This later becomes Freddie's solo line–which is silent with his mouth moving.)
We are fine.

Once the song is very familiar to all the students, I "advance" the "Hello, Freddie" song per grade level: Kindergarten sings it in unison; 1st grade, 2-part round; 2nd grade, 3-part round; 3rd grade, 4-part round, but not every class time. Each class enters and goes to their singing place. The grades singing in rounds stand in assigned circles. The circle that is "ready" first gets to start the round. After the song is finished, the students are now intrigued with this little stuffed frog that came to life. Freddie shakes his head and gets excited. He wants to tell his story. I tell Freddie that we do not have enough time to hear his story today. I ask the kids if they would like to hear his story the next time they come to music. Of course, they nod their heads with excitement. The next time that the students come to your class, they will be anticipating the story and have forgotten their fears of coming to a new room.

SPECIAL NOTE. Pretend that only you, the teacher, can "hear" Freddie's voice. The kids hear his voice on the audio CD. Using your voice for Freddie will make him less magical, or "real," in the kids' minds, because your voice will not match Freddie's voice on the audio CD. Here's how I set it up for the kids. I tell the kids that I took a trip to Treble Clef Island, where all the animals sing, talk, dance and play instruments. When Freddie came back with me to meet the kids, we discovered that only I could hear Freddie! So...you must need to take a trip to Treble Clef Island to be able to "hear" Freddie!

3 GOOD REASONS TO USE FREDDIE THIS WAY:

1. Freddie's voice remains consistent with the voice on the CD, so he seems more real. The "real" factor makes it magical for the kids. (Think Disneyland characters wandering around nodding/shaking their heads and gesturing, but not talking.)
2. Easier for the teacher.
3. If a substitute is teaching or a student moves to another school where the music teacher is using Freddie, then there is still consistency with the "voice" of Freddie, because it is only imagined and used the same way by each teacher.

I demonstrate and explain using Freddie on the video link, "Music Teachers Meet Freddie the Frog" at **www.K3MusicTeachers.com**

FROG WARNING

I should warn you that once the kids are introduced to Freddie the Frog, especially after the first story, the kids fall in love with Freddie and music class. They will look forward to coming to music to get to see Freddie and find out what he wants to play, sing and do that day. If you are detained at the door by another teacher or student, the class will already be singing the "Hello, Freddie" song to Freddie. Freddie always sits at the front of the room until needed. Using Freddie will make your job easier and your music class popular. The students will tell their parents all about Freddie. They will bring drawings, gifts, friends, and sometimes if you're lucky, chocolate to Freddie. When they see you in the local store, they will ask about Freddie. If you use Freddie the Frog and his stories in your classroom, it will transform the way you introduce lessons, stories, games and songs. They all become Freddie's ideas and you will find the wiggliest kids fully captivated by this little frog. Teaching lower elementary becomes incredibly rewarding and fun!

Lesson 2

INTRODUCING TREBLE CLEF NOTES

- "Hello, Freddie" song (from Lesson 1)
- *Freddie the Frog® and the Thump in the Night* Book/CD (see page 55)
- Setting up the story
- Review using the pages at the end of the book
- "Froggie Went A'Courtin'" (CD Track 4)
- "Eli's Hokey Pokey" (CD Track 5)

SING "HELLO, FREDDIE"

When new students arrive for their second music class, and they go to their assigned seat, I ask if they would like to sing Freddie's song. We start our class with the "Hello, Freddie" song that we learned last time.

FREDDIE'S STORY

Now it's time to hear Freddie's story as you turn the pages and the students follow along. The very first story should always be *Freddie the Frog® and the Thump in the Night* with the CD playing. The enclosed audio CD has the voice of Freddie and his best friend Eli, and the sound effects bring the story to life for the kids. While the story is playing (CD Tracks 1 & 2), you can demonstrate using two fingers to tap the *thump, thump, thump, thump* on their other hand.

At the end of the story, quickly review the characters and places introduced in the story on the staff with the question marks located in the last pages of the book. Then show the students the illustrated answers on the next page and review again.

MOVE TO THE BEAT

Ask the students to stand and move to the beat of "Froggie Went A'Courtin'" (CD Track 4). Form a large circle and do "Eli's Hokey Pokey" (CD Track 5). Pretend to have Freddie interrupt you and get your attention. He wants to know if he can give the kids a hug. I explain that not all the kids might want a hug and that's okay. Then I tell the students that if they can line up very quietly, they can give a hug to Freddie if they want to, but only those students standing in line quietly. As the students file out the door and into their room, they give Freddie a hug if wanted. (Most kids will want to and will look forward to this every music class.) Some will give him a "high five" instead.

By the end of this music lesson, the kids are in love with Freddie the Frog®. The story gave the puppet a personality and now he has truly become real. The kids are now connected and this connection is a key factor to everything else. Now the chosen puppet, Freddie the Frog®, becomes a wonderful tool for teaching music and more! Now use your magic tool that the kids come to see every single music class.

Lesson 3

DISCOVERING FREDDIE'S ABC'S (THE MUSIC ALPHABET)

- "Hello, Freddie" song
- A captivating cue set: The magic of a puppet
- Freddie's Name That Tune Game
- Review using *Thump in the Night* Flashcards (see page 55)
- Music stories on barred instruments

A CAPTIVATING CUE SET: THE MAGIC OF A PUPPET

Now that the students have a relationship with the puppet, it can become a fun tool for cue sets to introduce the concept of the day. Many times I greet the kids at the doorway of their classroom, and simply say, "Freddie has something exciting to show you today." Or maybe I will say, "Freddie has a game he wants to play today." By greeting the kids at their doorway, you already have their attention and focused anticipation of coming to your room. Once you're at your room, depending on what the lesson of the concept is that you want to teach that day, you might say that you have to do your job of listening or singing first before we get to play Freddie's game. One of those games is called "Name that Tune."

SING "HELLO, FREDDIE"

NAME THAT TUNE GAME—FREDDIE'S ALPHABET (THE MUSIC ALPHABET)

- Freddie wants to play "Name That Tune" game.
- Pretend that Freddie hums a tune to you, the teacher, and listen.
- Ask the students not to blurt out what they are hearing, but raise their hand. Hum the tune, "Twinkle, Twinkle, Little Star."
- Ask a student with a hand raised, what he/she thinks it is.
- Most students will guess "Twinkle, Twinkle, Little Star" first.
- Ask the students if they can sing that song.
- Freddie shakes his head and says that they are not finished.
- He wants to play again.
- He "hums" the same tune to me. I hum the same tune to the kids.
- He explains that there is another song with the same tune but different lyrics.
- The students discover two more songs, "Baa, Baa, Black Sheep," and the "ABC" song.
- When the students sing the ABC song, look really pleased until they get to the letter H. Have Freddie shake his head as though something is wrong, and stop the kids singing to ask what is the matter.
- Freddie explains that his alphabet is only seven letters long on Treble Clef Island--it only goes to "G"!
- Ask students if they would mind singing Freddie's alphabet in music class.

NOTE: This is an activity to repeat at the beginning of each year in first grade, second grade and third grade. It will refresh their memory, and be a fun way to review Freddie's alphabet, which is actually the music alphabet. At the first-, second- and third-grade levels, ask the students to sing Freddie's alphabet backwards. The audio CD that comes in *Freddie the Frog® and the Bass Clef Monster* includes music tracks with the music alphabet sung forward, backwards, and an accompaniment track to sing it whichever way you prefer. Mix it up to increase the challenge.

At this point, you have established Freddie's alphabet as the music alphabet to be used in the music classroom. You have also established six of the notes on the treble clef staff as characters, places or events that happened on the treble clef staff. The kids see the staff as a map of where Freddie lives, making it all fun and games. You, the teacher, know that it is a fun introduction to reading the music notes.

KID-FRIENDLY NOTE NAME REVIEW

The set of six flashcards that go with the **Thump in the Night** story (see page 55) is a great tool for quick review of those note names in a fun way. In 10 seconds or less, you can review with the kids, and we all know that repetition is important for retention. The first time you use the flashcards, present them to kids as though Freddie is worried that they will forget his story. Of course, the kids adamantly shake their heads that they would never forget his story. I relay that I told Freddie that, but he was not sure. Then I show the flashcards, and the students answer with the different character names or events that happened. From then on, it is quick and easy to show the flashcards, and the kids know what to do. The cards now may be used to choose kids for special jobs, special singing parts, special playing parts on instruments, etc.

FLASHCARDS AND BARRED INSTRUMENTS

Now that your students are comfortable with flashcards and understand what they mean, you can use the flashcards as your focal point for playing instruments with pitches. On a barred instrument, such as a xylophone, metallophone, or glockenspiel, I leave all of the bars on the instrument to demonstrate the correlation between the flashcards with the music notes and the pitches on the instruments. Holding out the two flashcards, line note F and space note F, I ask the kids to point to the note that looks higher. Then I ask them to point to the note that looks lower. I ask them what they are. They respond with Freddie's home and Freddie's vacation home. Then I point to the barred instrument and ask, "Did you know that Freddie's alphabet is on the barred instruments?" Freddie or I play the barred instrument starting with the letter A, and I sing the letters of the alphabet as I play. Then I ask, "Which F do you think is Freddie's home, and which is his vacation home?" The students guess and discover the correlation between the line F and the space F, establishing the sound of high and low, the octave, and the visual representation of the written high F and low F.

Now that the correlation between the flashcards and the actual notes on the barred instruments is established, help the students discover the other four note names on the flashcards and how they each correlate to a specific bar on the instrument. Now it's time to have some creative fun with what they've learned!

MUSIC STORIES ON BARRED INSTRUMENTS

Divide the class in half; one half plays on the letter F for Freddie's home, and the other half plays on the low E for Eli's home. Structure the activity by giving the students questions to ask verbally, and then played, as they verbalize on their note.

For example, the Freddie students could ask, "How are you?" while playing three quarter notes on the high F on the xylophone. The Eli students could answer, "I am fine" while playing three quarter notes on the low E.

Depending on your time schedule and the age of the students, you can build on this activity to a full composition, or just the simple activity described for younger students. Just remember that the focus of this activity is the correlation of the written note to the corresponding pitched bar on the instrument.

Lesson 4

INTRODUCING RHYTHM, BEAT AND TEMPO

- "Hello, Freddie" song
- *Freddie the Frog® and the Mysterious Wahooooo* Book/CD (see page 56)
- Setting up the story with mini-maracas and rhythm sticks
- Review using the Tempo Island Magnetic Rhythm Board Set (see page 56)

PREPARATION

Freddie the Frog® and the Mysterious Wahooooo is the second book I introduce. This gives the kids a chance to review the six notes that they learned in *The Thump in the Night*, and it immediately gets the kids involved in recognizing simple rhythm patterns, different tempo terms – and feeling the beat.

Kids love this book. It's fun and interactive. Teachers love this book because kids experience the difference between beat and rhythm, performing them simultaneously! It is easy for kids because they connect the terms beat and rhythm to visual and auditory characters in the story. At the end of the story, the students clearly understand the difference between these 2 terms simply by connecting to which character in the story represented beat, which is Eli the Elephant, and which character in the story represented rhythm, which is Freddie the Frog. They also experience and understand the tempo terms, *andante, allegro, largo, presto, accelerando* and *ritardando*.

SING "HELLO, FREDDIE"

SETTING UP THE STORY

Here is a helpful classroom management tool I use before beginning this story. I ask the students if they would like to play a rhythm instrument along with Freddie and Eli. Divide the class into two sections. One section will play the beat with Eli using rhythms sticks, chopsticks or unsharpened pencils. The other half of the class will use small shakers, such as mini-maracas or little egg shakers. I hand out the shakers and the rhythm sticks to the students and turn to pages 4 & 5 in the book where Eli is on the left and Freddie is on the right with a simple rhythm pattern made out of sticks. I prepare the children by explaining that when Eli starts to play the beat, the Eli students play the beat with him, and the students with the shakers play with Freddie when he plays the rhythm. When they hear the word, "fine," they are to stop. We practice doing what I just described. I instruct the "beat" kids to quietly say "ta" as they play along.

I ask the students if they should play loudly or softly and why. I also mention that if they forget and play their instrument too loudly or do something with it that they should not do, what do they think will happen? Of course, they will say it will get taken away. If one child does not do their job using their instrument responsibly, I quietly take it away, and then after a few minutes, look at them and quietly ask if they can do their job? Most of the time they nod their head and you quietly give it back without interrupting the story. Once students see that you will actually do what you said you would do, it's not a problem. Now it is time to begin.

BEYOND THE BOOKS – TEACHER GUIDE

THE STORY: Freddie the Frog® and The Mysterious Wahooooo

Put in the CD or turn on your iPod, push "play" and turn the pages. When you get to the Freddie and Eli pages, conduct the kids to play their part. When they hear, "fine," indicate to stop. At the end of the story, you may collect the instruments, or if you have time, extend the lesson with the Magnetic Rhythm Board of Tempo Island.

MAGNETIC RHYTHM BOARD

Create 4-count rhythm patterns with Freddie's Magnetic Rhythm Board (see page 56). This is a great way to do rhythm assessment and to introduce simple and successful composition. It's perfect for composing the four-count rhythm patterns in an efficient amount of time.

With the Largo rhythm track playing (CD Track 5, **The Mysterious Wahooooo**), ask a student to come up and pick a magnet and place it on one of the four marked counts on the magnet board. Then ask that student or the class to say the new rhythm pattern, then play it with the rhythm instrument that is still in their hand. Depending on your class, you may have collected their instruments and they may chant it instead, or play the one instrument that you have at the front while they chant. Keep the audio track playing and quickly point to someone else to come up and take his or her turn. Repeat the process of having that child, or the class, chant the new rhythm pattern and then repeat it a few times with their instruments or by chanting. See the helpful "magnetic" instructions that come with the rhythm board.

ASSESSMENT

If you use this as an assessment, have a checklist off to the side, and score each child as they chant the rhythm pattern they created. For young students, this might be their first simple composition. They love hearing what they just created. If it works well in your situation, the magnetic rhythm board is also an online game located at www.FreddieTheFrog.com. Click on the GAMES tab and then click on the picture of the magnetic board located below **The Mysterious Wahooooo** book image. I do this game online in class at least once a year, so they understand how to find it at home on the Internet and how to play it using the computer. It's important to teach how to get to the site and demonstrate it in class so they can find it independently at home. Many kids talk about playing the games at home. What a great way to reinforce the learning that is going on in your room.

Lesson 5

COMPOSING 4-BEAT RHYTHM PATTERNS

- "Hello, Freddie" Song
- The Tempo Game!
- Craft Sticks

SING "HELLO, FREDDIE"

THE TEMPO GAME!

Freddie wants to play a game. My kids and I absolutely love this next game. It's very simple and fun, it's a great classroom management tool, and they learn their tempo terms! The first time we play, I ask the students to stand. Then I boldly say, "Andante!"

I wait. They look at me wondering what that word means, and so I continue.

"Move like a queen or king in their palace," I say, and I fold my hands formally in front of me and stand tall as I move at a nice walking tempo through our pretend palace.

Then I firmly and boldly say, "Fine!"

I say it in the similar way as I would say, "freeze," and that's exactly what they do. I share that we have magical musical words that, only if you are in music, you know what they mean. "Andante" means to walk very politely around the room and "Fine" means to stop and pretend it's the end, standing with feet together and hands at your side.

Then I say, "Pretend that you are really happy today and it is sunny and warm outside. Skip or walk very quickly. Allegro!"

They begin to skip until I say, "Fine."

Then I say, "Largo!" I ask the students to take large and slow steps.

Then I say, "Fine."

Now I tell them that if we were outside in the recess playground and they could run as fast as they wanted over the grass, that would be this word, but since we are inside with lots of things to run into, we will have to do this word running in place.

"Presto!" They run in place. They love this one!

Then I say, "Fine."

This is a requested game by students and is a great game for when they seem to be a bit off task or restless and you're having trouble getting them to focus. Just quickly say, "Allegro," and point the direction that you want them to move in the room. I direct them to move in a circular fashion in the same direction. They may pass but they can't touch or talk, and if they do, they're out of the game.

TEACHER TIP: If you can make students move, you immediately regain control of the classroom. Just simply make them move and you naturally become the leader of the room once again.

EXTEND THE TEMPO GAME

You can enhance this game in multiple ways. For example, add a hand drum or different instrument that plays the beat of the named tempo. The students have to move to that beat or they are out. You can also choose students to choose the tempo and play the instrument for the class to move to.

Another version my kids love is switching between "Fine" or "freeze" for stopping. It forces them to know the difference between these 2 words. "Fine" means to stop with your feet together, standing tall with your hands at your side. "Freeze" means to stop in place, frozen like a statue. If the leader says, "freeze" but someone stands in a "Fine" position, then they're out and have to sit down. If you say "Fine" and they "freeze," then they're out and they have to sit down. Once a student is out, they become part of the team of judges, and nobody can argue with the judge! If you choose to argue the judge, you are out. This takes care of a lot of arguments.

Like any good game, you can continue to add your own additions and changes to make it your very own. Because of this game, a very high percentage of my students know the tempo terms used in the game. When we are analyzing or listening to music, I ask them to describe that music using tempo and dynamic terms. This is easy for them to do because of the stories and games we play in the classroom. The more your students experience music concepts, the more that they can use the concepts in other ways.

TEACHER NOTE: My whole teaching philosophy is based on students needing to experience the concepts to give them meaning. We need to constantly strive to do less talking and more doing in our teaching. We all remember things that we actively participate in far more than what we read and learn. The beauty of teaching music to young kids is that "doing" means playing, and playing means learning.

4-COUNT RHYTHM PATTERNS WITH CRAFT STICKS

Since the birds use sticks to create rhythm patterns in this story, it is easy for students to transfer creating their own rhythm patterns using craft sticks, or Popsicle sticks. This is excellent for first notation writing in a format that young students do with success. Using craft sticks, I ask the students how could I make *ta* (quarter note) with sticks. Of course, that is the easiest thing to make by simply laying one craft stick vertically up and down. I draw *ti-ti* (two eighth notes) on the board and ask how many sticks does it take to make *ti-ti*? The students count and answer, three. I demonstrate and then have the students make *ti-ti*. The next step is turning *ti-ti* into *tika-tika* (four sixteenth notes). I teach them to make *ti-ti* first, then add two more sticks vertically up and down inside the *ti-ti* and one more across the top horizontally to make the four sixteenth note set. Finally, I demonstrate making a quarter rest using three craft sticks that looks similiar to a slanted "S". *(Refer to the stick rhythm notation in The Mysterious Wahooooo book for clarification. Stick rhythm notation included via Digital Access is used in digital documents, such as Smartboard files.)*

The core curriculum emphasizes teaching all content areas within other content areas. Using craft sticks to create rhythm patterns provides a great opportunity to introduce algebra, counting, patterns and other math concepts. Rhythm patterns are full of patterns, thus the name.

The first time students use the craft sticks to make a rhythm pattern, I guide them by asking them how many "things" there will be in a pattern. Using the storybook as a guide (see page 5, for example), they will answer, four. You and I know there are many different amounts that you could have, but to keep it simple, I start with a base of always having four things, or four counts, in a rhythm pattern. In the beginning, it's less confusing for the kids to use the word "things," instead of "counts", as in, four things in a rhythm pattern. Using the word "counts" automatically means counting and that is confusing when you're holding a bunch of sticks in your hands and talking about counting in the general classroom. If I say how many things and point to a rhythm pattern in the book, they quickly can see the four different things, although we know it as counts. Then I ask them to make a specific pattern that I dictate, such as, "ta, ta, ti-ti, ta." I quickly glance to assess successful task completion, and then I ask the students to use their index finger and chant it with me, following along with their own pattern from left to right. You can visually assess any students that need additional help, and give silent individual help by pointing with them as the class chants the rhythm pattern. This task also helps the skill of reading left to right.

I ask the students to make another rhythm pattern with four things in it, and it cannot be the same as their neighbor's pattern. This gets the creative juices flowing and they have fun making their own creative rhythm pattern.

If the students are grouped in a circle or long lines, then I point to the first student's pattern and we chant together, moving to the next student in line until it sounds like a rhythm pattern piece. If the instruments are still close by, we can now play that rhythm pattern piece with instruments. The tempo tracks from **The Mysterious Wahooooo** CD named largo (Tr. 5), andante (Tr. 6) and allegro (Tr. 7) are perfect to accompany the class rhythm pattern piece because it is chanted and played with non-pitched classroom instruments.

Now we can take it to the next level and create patterns with the four-count rhythm patterns. I suggest that every other rhythm pattern be the same one. For example if there were 20 kids in the room, then all of the odd numbered kids would change their pattern to "ta, ta, ti-ti, ta." The even-numbered kids can keep their patterns the way they are. Now we chant in the row as we did before, but this time they will hear the recurring pattern and it will begin to sound more like a real piece rather than unending rhythms. We discuss how the patterns make it sound more like a piece of music.

INTRODUCING MEASURES WITH RECTANGLE BOXES

When primary students begin to read rhythm patterns, the *ta* (quarter note) is typically a single vertical line. So when we draw measures of music on the board using *ta, ti-ti* and bar lines, the bar lines are confusing and the kids have difficulty knowing if it is a *ta* or a bar line. Therefore, in the beginning I draw rectangular boxes on the board to represent each measure. I choose to use rectangular boxes because those look so similar to flash cards with rhythm patterns on them. In fact, because I use boxes and rhythm cards in rectangular shapes, I never have to explain that each one is a measure.

Once the students are older and very comfortable with the rectangular boxes and how many "things" go in each box, then I simply show them that instead of drawing the entire rectangular box, I'll just draw that line and it means the same thing. Because they've used boxes for so long, switching to just one line is no longer confusing as a quarter note. This saves you a lot of time and headache.

FLASHCARD REVIEW

As the students stand and turn in a line ready to exit, do a quick review of **The Thump in the Night** flashcards before leaving class.

Lesson 6

THE 12-BAR BLUES CHORD PROGRESSION
- "Hello, Freddie" Song
- Create Rhythm Patterns to the 12-Bar Blues
- Add Boomwhackers

PREPARATION

The next lesson is a great time to create a class song with 12 measures in it. I begin by drawing 12 boxes on the board. We revisit what we learned about patterns, and how patterns make it sound like a piece of music. I "number" each box with a Roman numeral to show a chord progression in this order: I, I, I, I, IV, IV, I, I, V, IV, I, I.

TEACHER NOTE: If you can project files from your computer, you can incorporate a step-by-step visual display of the following lesson by using the "12-Bar Blues" PDF file *available via Digital Access*.

SING "HELLO, FREDDIE"

COMPOSE 4-COUNT RHYTHM PATTERNS

After singing the "Hello, Freddie" song, I ask the kids if they know what a secret message is? Explain that what you have drawn on the board is kind of like a secret message of music. If we can decode it, we get to play it. I guide them through discovering what each of the Roman numerals stand for. I ask for a student to create a rhythm pattern to put in one of the boxes up on the board. To keep things simple and make it very visual for the kids to see the difference when the chords change, I write the newly created rhythm pattern in all of the boxes with the same chord name. For example, if a student chose to write *ta, ta, ti-ti, ta* in measure one for the I chord, then I would guide the students to tell me to write that same rhythm pattern in every box labeled "I."

Now I ask another student to pick a different rhythm pattern for the IV chord and we put that pattern in every box labeled "IV". Now we ask one more student to create a rhythm pattern for the V chord box, which in the beginning 12-bar blues, only happens in one box.

ADD BOOMWHACKERS

Now I add the Boomwhackers. Boomwhackers are great because they are different colors and very visual, fun to play, and they are pitched. I also like the Boomwhackers because they each have the pitch letter written on them.

My next question to the students is how do we know which of the Boomwhackers to play for which measure, or box? Here's the fun part. We get to help them discover chord progressions.

I then ask the students, "What is Freddie's alphabet?" They quickly answer A, B, C, D, E, F and G. I write those letters on the board and then ask what would come before the A and what would come after the G? I put a few more letters in front of and behind Freddie's alphabet, and then I say, "I'm going to choose the letter A as number I." I write a number "I" under the letter A.

Then I go on to say, "If A is I, what do you think is number IV?" It usually takes a few guesses, but eventually they figure out it is the letter D. Once that is discovered, I ask, "So what is V?" Now it's easy and everyone understands that it is E.

I erase the Roman numeral I under the letter A and write the Roman numeral I under the C. I ask, "If C is I, then what is IV?" Now they understand, so they quickly answer the letter F. I ask, "What is V?" They answer G.

Now I choose the Boomwhackers with the letters C, F and G. I ask them to listen while I play what they have written. Using just the Boomwhackers and the rhythm patterns that the students created, I play the 12-bar blues, softly chanting the chord progression number at the beginning of each measure. The kids are in awe of the progression that they have just heard. Now they are excited and they want to play.

CHORDS WITH BOOMWHACKERS

Depending on the age of your students and how much time you have in a class period, you can add another note. If you're ready to go to the next step, you can simply say that there are certain notes that go with the chosen letters that make it sound good together. In chord format on the board, I write the letter E above the C, the letter A above the F, and the letter B above the G so they are introduced to the sound and chord spelling visual. One set of students get the C and E, and I tell them to play the rhythm patterns for the I chord. Another set of students get the F and A and play the rhythm pattern for the IV chord. The last set of students get G, B and D and play the rhythm pattern for the V chord. I instruct the students to play when it is their turn in the chord progression. Now we play the rhythms patterns with the kids playing and hearing the chords and the chord progression. They are experiencing and hearing the sound of the 12-bar chord blues progression and understanding the very basics of how it fits together!

EXPAND AND IMPROVISE

To expand this lesson even further, you can have a set of xylophones or glockenspiel set up with the notes of the corresponding scale and you, the teacher, can model improvising a melody while the class plays the chord progression.

Lesson 7

CALL AND RESPONSE ON PITCHED INSTRUMENTS

- "Hello, Freddie" song
- 4-Count Melodic Improvisation
- Call and Response

SING "HELLO, FREDDIE"

SET-UP

If you have sets of barred instruments in your room, this is a great time to teach echo, call and response and melodic notes that fit together in a chord structure. Since you have already talked about notes of the chords that go together (end of Lesson 6), you can guide students into melodic improvisation. Prior to the lesson, draw 12 "measure boxes" on the board in 3 rows of 4, and label each box with either the Roman numeral I, IV or V to show the 12-bar blues pattern from Lesson 6. With 1 or 2 student(s) per instrument, set students up in 6 pairs, and assign each pair one of these 3 chord numerals. The exception will be the one pair for the V and IV chords at the beginning of the third line. If you only have 3 barred instruments, student pairs can share an instrument. In my case, I have lots of glockenspiels, so I place 12 students on 12 glockenspiels, either in pairs around the room, preferably in a line, or on the floor with the glockenspiels set up to mirror the 12-bar blues pattern on the board—three lines of four glockenspiels, one student at each one. Point out that they are set up like the boxes on the board, and the students will make the connection themselves.

1st Pair: I	I	2nd Pair: I	I
3rd Pair: IV	IV	4th Pair: I	I
5th Pair: V	IV	6th Pair: I	I

ECHO IMPROV

Depending on ability, have students play either 1-note or 2-note chords for this activity. Using the Key of C, review with students assigned to the I chord, what notes they would play (C and E); IV chord students – F and A; and V chord students – G and B. The first 2 "boxes" are for the 1st pair assigned to the I chord. When I point to Box 1, one partner makes up and plays a 4-count rhythm pattern using the notes in his/her chord. Box 2, the other partner echos that pattern. Boxes 3 & 4 are for the 2nd pair of partners assigned to the I chord, and so on. When you get to the V chord and IV chord measures, have the first partner make up a pattern on his/her V chord notes, then the second partner echos the pattern on his/her IV chord notes. Add other students playing one or more ostinati patterns using Boomwhackers and classroom instruments to create the "rhythm section." Rotate students so they each get to play the various parts.

CALL AND RESPONSE

Once the students are comfortable and understand echoing a melodic pattern, we can become a little more creative. Have the first partner "ask a question" by making up and playing any 4-count rhythm pattern on their note(s). Their partner "answers" with a new pattern on their note(s). I teach this by using actual verbal questions that they play on the notes. Simple things like, "How are you?" And the partner answers, "I am fine." Then I ask the first partner to ask a different question that they make up. Before playing it, I give them a chance to verbally ask the question and the partner to verbally answer the question. Now we put it to music by playing the question/answer on the assigned notes.

When the students reach a nice comfort level with this step, add another note to their chord of options. This can continue on until students have four or five notes to choose from. This would definitely be something that you would do over several lessons, and it would depend on the age and size of your group, how far you could go and what you could do. The options are endless.

If you have time, try the same lesson in a different key helping the kids hear different sounds in different keys, such as E for great pentatonic melodic improv on E, G, A, B, D. The key of G works well on the xylophones, using the extra bars F♯ and B♭ to add some blues notes. For the purposes of this book, it's time to move on. If you're reading this book, most of you are working with younger primary age kids. Most likely, with young kids, you will stick to just one or two notes for the kids to echo, or call and respond.

ASSESSING RHYTHM, TEMPO AND BEAT

There are several ways to assess beat, tempo and rhythm patterns.

- Students could create four-count rhythm patterns with craft sticks.
- You hold up a rhythm pattern card and students chant it to you.
- You say a tempo word and they can move at the correct speed.
- You play a piece of music and they identify which tempo it is they are hearing by circling a picture of an animal moving at that tempo.

You can also assess students by creating new rhythm patterns using the magnetic rhythm board and having them chant it back. Rhythm patterns are one of the easiest concepts to assess in a group setting and have evidence of individual comprehension and competence.

Lesson 8

INTRODUCING BASS CLEF NOTES

- "Hello, Freddie" song
- **Freddie the Frog® and the Bass Clef Monster** Book/CD and Poster (see page 56)
- Freddie's ABCs – forwards and backwards! (CD Tracks 4 - 7)
- "Hop 'N Flop Shuffle" (CD Track 8)

SING "HELLO, FREDDIE"

A NEW FREDDIE STORY

I announce that Freddie has a new story he would like to share, and then ask the students to raise their hand if they've ever had a scary dream. They will want to share their scary dreams, but quickly stop them and apologize, and tell them that Freddie had a scary dream, and he would love to share his dream. If we listen to everybody's scary dream, we won't have time to hear his. I ask if it would be okay if we listen to his story? Young kids will eagerly agree.

Before I begin the story, I pretend that Freddie is talking to me. He tells me that he is really glad that it was just a dream and not real. I turn to the students and say, "Aren't you glad that, when you have a scary dream, you wake up and realize that it's not real?"

Then I share with the students that this was a scary dream and Freddie was really glad that it was not real. Freddie is nodding his head emphatically. Then I open the book, push play on the CD and turn the pages. **The Bass Clef Monster** story introduces nine bass clef notes. At the end of the story, we review with the staff pages at the end of the book. In subsequent lessons, we use the flashcards to do a quick review.

BASS CLEF IN KINDERGARTEN?

Sharing the bass clef story is very easy. The bigger question is, when do you share it and should you share it? There are several teachers that disagree with introducing and teaching the bass clef until children are older. I disagree. I come from a background of teaching piano creatively to young children. If kindergarten students can learn dinosaur names, they can certainly learn bass clef notes. I have taught children from ages three through college-age students for over 20 years. I have never had a problem with children being too confused with treble clef notes and bass clef notes. In fact, the bass clef story is often their favorite story. The key is in how you as a teacher set it up, how you introduce concepts, and how you take it to the next step.

The Freddie stories make the connection in a visual way that makes sense to kids and helps to keep the differences separated. The stories give reference points to hook back to and build upon. Talking about those differences at a young age makes it so much easier when they are older. My kindergarten students look for the Bass Clef Monster or Treble Clef Island on the flashcard to know which note it is. How wonderful for the student who is older to already know that difference effortlessly!

There are some that feel that unless you are playing or hearing the matching pitch that goes with the written note, that you are doing harm. Again, I disagree. It's all how you teach them, from what philosophy you are coming from, and how you deliver it and teach it to the children. We use bass xylophones, alto xylophones, soprano glockenspiels and pianos so they hear music notes from both the treble clef and the bass clef.

That is just my theory and my background of teaching. Each teacher needs to teach what they are comfortable with, as long as the child is being taught, and we all reach the same goal. The most important thing is that we teach children with passion. They'll all get to the same end result if we understand where we are coming from, where we are going with the concepts, and do it all with passion and a deep sense of why we are doing what we do.

One of the reasons that I love to teach both the bass clef and treble clef is because it also introduces the music alphabet. Previously I described how Freddie introduced the game, "Name That Tune," and the students discover Freddie's alphabet. At the end of **The Bass Clef Monster** story, I ask the students if they can see Freddie's alphabet on the illustrated staff at the end. Sometimes they discover it before I've even asked the question. It is the perfect time to point and show Freddie's alphabet outlined on the bass clef illustrated staff in the book or on the poster.

LESSON EXTENSION ON PITCHED INSTRUMENTS

If you have bass clef xylophones, a piano in your room or another pitched instrument that uses the bass clef notes, then definitely spend some time demonstrating and interacting the correlation between the bass cleff flashcards and the pitches on those pitched instruments. It will be well worth the time spent for the students to hear the sound of the notated bass clef note.

Play similar games to those outlined for the treble clef pitched instruments. You can easily structure creating stories on the pitched instruments using the flashcards with the corresponding character or event on that pitched note. For example, Annie the Ant on the line A could have a conversation with another student who is playing their piece of the conversation on the D for the Dragon. The kids have a lot of fun creating stories between a dragon and an ant. Not only is this great for identifying the sound that goes with the visual representation of it, it is also very cross-curricular and creative. You can easily guide students to create stories with a simple introduction, plot, climax and solution ending that can be transferred to the pitched instruments on the corresponding notes. Create sound effects with other classroom instruments, create an ostinati, and have fun.

FREDDIE'S ABCS FORWARDS AND BACKWARDS

Now that the students have discovered Freddie's ABCs in the back of the Bass Clef Monster story, use the four soundtracks on **The Bass Clef Monster** CD. Track #4 is Freddie and Eli suggesting that they sing Freddie's ABCs and the kids naturally jump in and sing with them. Eli then asks if they can sing it reggae style (track #5), which is really fun for the kids. It is especially nice for kindergarten kids since the reggae style ABCs actually slows the singing of each letter down just a bit while having more fun singing. I add simple movements of rolling my arms and sticking a fist in the air for every letter in a fun, reggae style. Then Eli or Freddie suggests that they sing it backwards, reggae style (track #6). This is a great step.

The skill of recognizing the musical alphabet forwards and backwards really helps the students when they begin reading music. By introducing it as simply a game or song that Freddie and Eli want to play, there is no pressure for the kids. I make it a game by asking the kids to dictate how to write Freddie's alphabet on the board backwards. As the students begin to sing it, I erase one letter at a time until they are singing it backwards without seeing it on the board. If they are feeling pretty confident, they sing the alphabet backwards with the accompaniment soundtrack (track #7). I challenge the students by playing a game and asking them to sing it forwards or backwards on my command throughout the song. Of course, you do not want to do this until you know that they're comfortable singing backwards.

The same soundtrack would fit with any of the tunes that go with the ABC song. So it can be used as an accompaniment for "Twinkle, Twinkle, Little Star," "Ba, Ba, Black Sheep" or the regular "ABC" song.

HOP 'N FLOP SHUFFLE

- Ask the kids to spread out and find their own space, looking at you.
- Grab a guitar from the sky.
- Start the song, "Hop 'N Flop Shuffle" (CD Track #8). Kids LOVE it!
- 1st verse. Pretend to strum the electric guitar with the beat of the music.
- 2nd verse. Turn your arms into elephant ears by holding on to your human ears with your fingers. This transforms your arms into a V-shaped elephant ear. Flap your elephant ears to the beat.
- Chorus. Air guitar or elephant ears. Your choice.
- Coda. Strum the guitar and go down to one knee for a showy electric air guitar finish.

Show **The Bass Clef Monster** poster and display in the room.

COLORING PAGES

There are nine coloring pages that are free, downloadable and reproducible at www.FreddieTheFrog.com. Each coloring page has an image from the book and a picture of the music note on a staff to reinforce the correlation.

Lesson 9

INTRODUCTION TO SOLFEGE (DO, RE, MI) AND CLEF SIGNS

- "Hello, Freddie" Song
- Freddie's Mystery Singing Game and introduction to Solfege (*do, re, mi*) using "The Closet Key"
- Identifying the difference between the treble clef and bass clef signs
- Review using **Bass Clef Monster** and **Thump in the Night** flashcards (see pages 55 & 56)

PREPARATION

Before the students enter the room, draw four rectangles on the board. Each rectangle represents a measure. Number the rectangles 1-4, and draw the rhythm patterns to "Closet Key." Place the rhythmic notation melodically (up and down). Draw as shown below. If you can project files from your computer, show the 1st page of "The Closet Key" PDF file available via Digital Access.

SING "HELLO, FREDDIE"

Freddie's Mystery Singing Game (and introduction to solfege)

Tell the kids that Freddie wrote a mystery song on the board and if they can figure it out, they get to play the game!

Lead them through the following steps, discovering solfege *do, mi,* and *re* along the way.

Step 1. Ask the students to chant the rhythm beginning in box 1, and continue on through 2, 3, 4.

Step 2. Ask the students if they see a pattern. Which two boxes are the same? (1 & 3) Which two boxes are different? (2 & 4) Why? (Lead them to seeing that the last note in these two boxes goes in different directions. One goes up, the other goes down.)

Step 3. Tell the students there are special singing words that help us learn the melody. Demonstrate that the first two notes in Box 1 are "do's," so you are going to write a "d" under each one of those notes because "do" begins with "d." The third and fourth notes are "mi's," so you are going to write "m's" under each of them.

Step 4. Ask the kids what letter should you write under notes 5 & 6? ("d's" for do)

Step 5. Continue on until you get to the "re" in box 2. Explain that it is "re," so you will put an "r" there.

Step 6. Ask what letter you should put under the last note in box 2. (m)

Step 7. Ask the kids if they can finish telling you what letters to put underneath each note in Boxes 3 & 4.

Step 8. Echo sing each box if it is the students' first time to experience solfege (kindergarten). Ask if any student can sing it without hearing it sung by you, the teacher, if it is an older class that is comfortable with solfeggio.

BEYOND THE BOOKS – TEACHER GUIDE

Step 9. Entire class sings the song in solfege without the teacher singing. Once sung successfully, ready for the last step.

Step 10. Now sing the lyrics.

RULES OF THE GAME:

- One student closes their eyes. (I usually send the student to a corner of the room to close and cover his or her eyes.)
- Another student is given a physical key to hide anywhere in the room, but at least a part of the key has to be showing. When finished hiding the key, the student returns to his or her seat.
- We sing "The Closet Key" song while the student looks for the key. The only clue we can give is with our singing voices. If the student is far away from the hiding place, we sing softly. As he or she moves closer to the key, we sing louder.
- Once the student realizes she or he is in the "hot spot," I announce "Level 2."
- Level 2 means the student is in the correct spot. We change our singing volume to reflect when the student is looking in the right direction of the hiding spot or not.
- Once the key is found. Two new players get a turn.

Kids LOVE this game and want to play it often. It is great for learning how to control their singing voice, matching pitch, singing expressively as a group and having fun!

TEACHER NOTE: This game is wonderful to use on those special days close to holidays. The last day before Christmas break, Freddie introduces it as a mystery song again. When they discover that it is the closet key game, I say that since it is Christmas time, let's hide jingle bells instead and change the words to the following:

I have lost my jingle bells in my Santa's workshop.

Or at Valentine's Day time it can become:

I have lost my valentine in my music classroom.

Review using **Bass Clef Monster** and **Thump in the Night** flashcards

About five minutes prior to the end of class, I pull out the **Bass Clef Monster** flashcards. Freddie's worried that they will forget his scary dream. Similar to the **Thump in the Night** flashcard review, the **Bass Clef Monster** flashcards come in very handy for quick review of the bass clef notes. We review the **Bass Clef Monster** story and then I point out the differences between the bass clef flashcards and the treble clef flashcards. I hold one of each in my hand and ask students to tell me what differences they see. When they point out the symbol of the treble clef island versus the bass clef monster, I instruct them that, yes, that is definitely the difference and you can always count on looking for that difference to know whether it's the **Bass Clef Monster** story or the **Thump in the Night** story.

We play a quick game with treble clef flashcards and bass clef flashcards mixed together. I ask them to simply identify bass clef or treble clef, rather than the note name. This really reinforces the concept to look at clef sign first. Once I see that the students can easily recognize the clef difference, we start identifying the actual notes by the character, place, or event in the corresponding story.

ASSESSMENT

I use the bass clef flashcards as well as the treble clef flashcards as quick reviews multiple times throughout the year. I try to use them at least once every two weeks as a very quick review or to choose people for different jobs. That way when it is assessment time, seeing the flashcards is very natural and comfortable for the students. I choose to assess the kids with the note name flashcards as part of my individual one-on-one assessment time. This way I know they understand the concept and the ability to identify the note with the flashcard.

Lesson 10

INTRODUCING MORE TREBLE CLEF NOTES

- "Hello, Freddie" Song
- *Freddie the Frog® and the Secret of Crater Island* Book/CD (see page 55)
- Review using *Secret of Crater Island* Flashcards (see page 55)
- Discovering the stories on the grand staff

SING "HELLO, FREDDIE"

ANOTHER FREDDIE STORY

After the students have sung "Hello, Freddie," Freddie gets excited and wants to share another story – *The Secret of Crater Island*. **TEACHER NOTE:** I intentionally wait until the students are confident identifying the six notes of the treble clef from *The Thump in the Night* story before introducing six more notes.

I open the book, start the audio track on the CD, and turn the pages. When the story is finished, I point at the staff in the back of the book without the illustrated pictures, and ask the students to tell me which bug did Freddie see first, then next, who wanted to eat the bugs, whom did Eli take them to meet, where did the Dolphins take them, and what was on Crater Island. Then I show them the next page with the illustrated answers. We might review it two or three times until I feel the students understand that each location represents specific pieces of the story.

This is a great time to point out that all of the bugs in the Freddie stories are line notes. I also point to the other places on the staff to help the kids make the correlation that the notes from *The Thump in the Night* fit on the same staff. I turn to the illustration of Treble Clef Island on the back cover, and beginning at the top, point out all the characters and places from both books, ending with the blowhole.

FLASHCARD REVIEW

The first time I use *The Secret of Crater Island* flashcards, I ask the students to identify if it is a line note or space note. I remind the students that the insects or bugs in the Freddie stories are all line notes.

LESSON EXTENSION ON PITCHED INSTRUMENTS

This activity is similar to the music stories we did with *The Thump in the Night*. Divide the students into partners; one will be a damselfly and the other will be a beetle bug. Then assign the partners to the glockenspiel, xylophones or other pitched instruments you have in your room. Hold up the flashcards, and help structure a conversation between the two bugs, playing their conversation on the corresponding note on their pitched instrument.

Once again, this is a fun and important way for the students to correlate what the visual representation of the written note name sounds like on the pitched instrument. Since they have done this activity before with *The Thump in the Night*, setting it up and understanding what to do this time will be very easy.

THE GRAND STAFF

Now you are ready to put it all together with the grand staff. I draw the treble clef staff on the board. Since we just finished ***The Secret of Crater Island*** book, I start by asking the kids to tell me where to place the different characters on that staff. For example, I point to the fourth line and ask what should go there. They say damselflies, so I write a D in the whole note on the fourth line. Then I go to the third line and ask what should go there. They answer the beetle bugs, so I place a B inside the whole note on the third line. I keep placing the characters and places from ***The Secret of Crater Island*** book on the treble clef staff at a diagonal, starting at the right side and working downward left.

Now I ask them to think about ***The Thump in the Night*** story and ask which line does Freddie live on. They answer the top line and I put an F inside the whole note at the right-hand side on the top line. I keep asking for other characters and places from ***The Thump in the Night***, filling in the answers at a diagonal on the treble clef staff. When we are finished, we have 12 labeled whole notes going at a diagonal from lower left to upper right with the combination of ***The Thump in the Night*** story and ***The Secret of Crater Island*** story.

I draw the bass clef staff underneath the treble clef staff. Starting at the bottom left-hand corner, I ask what happened in the dream. We begin with the gate, filling in the G inside the whole note on the bottom line and continue diagonally to the right and up with each piece of the dream. When I finish, I have drawn the grand staff and the notes so that it looks like one single diagonal line from lower left to top right. Now I ask how many times they can see Freddie's alphabet in the diagonal line.

With the whole grand staff in front of the students, you can show how the music alphabet repeats over and over and over. I demonstrate on the piano how it starts with the letter A and repeats the alphabet all the way up the keys. I point out where the written G begins on the piano and where Freddie's home is located on the piano, correlating to the written line F on the treble clef.

Putting the grand staff together along with the stories puts the pieces together for the kids and gives them ways to logically see, remember and read note names on the staff that make sense to them.

Now they have two ways to identify music notes on the staff. If they forget a piece of the story, they can use the alphabet to find the missing piece. Later in third grade, we make the transition and show not only the story and Freddie's alphabet, but the simple mnemonics. The universal line-note sentence, Every Good Boy Does Fine, and the spaces spelling, "FACE."

I changed the bass clef sentence to coordinate with the bass clef story. I teach Great Big Dragons Fear Ants for the line notes, and All Cows Eat Grass for the spaces. This ties it to the bass clef book and it helps the students keep the two staff mnemonics separate. It also helps the students keep the sentences mentally organized by remembering that the treble clef sentences are about a boy and his face; the bass clef sentences are about animals. I pretend each hand represents the treble and bass clef staves and line them up above each other with the fingers representing the lines and the spaces in between the fingers represent the spaces on the staff.

Show the Treble Clef poster (see page 55) and display in the room.

Lesson 11

COMPOSING A 12-BAR BLUES SONG
- "Hello, Freddie" Song
- Simple blues song composition
- Review note names using all of the flashcards

PREPARATION

Within **The Secret of Crater Island** story, there are blue beetle bugs that sing the blues to the kids. On the CD that is included with the book, there is an open blues track (Track #6) in the key of C, allowing lesson extensions for the class to create their own blues.

If the students have already discovered and created the 12-bar blues chord progression in previous lessons, then this sound will be familiar to them. If you have not done so, then this is a great time to learn the 12-bar chord progression (Lesson 6, pages 16-17). Once the students have gone through the process of creating a 12-bar blues chord progression with instruments, they are ready to create their own lyrics and melody. By creating their own lyrics and melody, they are experiencing what those two words actually mean.

SING "HELLO, FREDDIE"

COMPOSE A SIMPLE BLUES SONG

Give a brief explanation of the origin of the blues in American history, and how this style of music continues to be about something that folks are "blue" or sad about. The blue beetle bugs were blue about the Geckos keeping them from following the damselflies to Crater Island. I write the words of the "Gecko Blues" on the board, pointing out the rhyming words and the pattern. Now it is your students' turn to write a blues song. Brainstorm with them to come up with ideas of things that make them blue, such as getting sick or missing recess. Then I guide the students in replacing the "Gecko Blues" words with their words using the structure of the "Gecko Blues," remembering to include rhyming words at the end of every other line. Using the same tune as The Gecko Blues, here is an example of a blues song one of my classes composed on a rainy day.

THE GECKO BLUES

We won't see the secret.
No way. No how.
Those two hungry geckos
Want to eat us right now.

They're in the azaleas
Lookin' mighty foul.
But those damselflies sure are pretty.
We've gotta get there somehow.

We've got the Gecko, The Gecko,
The Gecko blues.
We've got the Gecko, The Gecko,
The Gecko blues.
We've got the Gecko, The Gecko,
The Gecko blues.

THE RAINY DAY RECESS BLUES

We don't get to go outside.
No way. No how.
It's thundering and lightning
And raining right now.

I hope it dries off soon
and the storm clouds go away.
But until the sun comes out
We're stuck inside all day.

We've got the rainy, the rainy day,
The rainy day recess blues.

We've got the rainy, the rainy day,
The rainy day recess blues.

We've got the rainy, the rainy day,
The rainy day recess blues.

Once the lyrics are complete, we decide if we want to keep the same melody as the Gecko blues or change it. I structure the changing so that it still has the blues sound. This is a great time to discuss possibly going up in the melody instead of going down. At K-3 level, I use melodic lines to show going up or down rather than drawing whole notes for the first draft. Depending if it is kindergarten or the third grade, I may transfer their melody into written staff music and then point out the correlation between the written melodic lines.

Now that the lyrics and melody are written, or at least decided upon, we practice singing our newly composed melody and lyrics. If the students seem ready, we put on the open blues track (CD Track #6) from **The Secret of Crater Island** and sing our blues. They just composed their first blues song and it was easy and fun!

If you are working with third, fourth, fifth, or sixth grade students, this is a great time to take it to the next step. Using the same process that you just modeled in class as a group, prepare a worksheet, with the structure outlined, so all they have to do is fill in the blank with their own newly created blues song words. If they want to change the melodic line, they can do so by just drawing that line to show when it goes up and down, and then singing it. If your class is advanced, you can actually have parts of the melody written on the staff, with parts of it open so the students can fill in and make changes. This is a lesson that can continue to spiral as far as you want to go. It is a great opportunity for music history, how it relates to other events in history and art, composition and solo singing.

Lesson 12 — MATCHING GAME WITH NOTE NAME FLASHCARDS

- "Hello, Freddie" Song
- 2 sets of each of the three flashcard sets

SING "HELLO, FREDDIE"

MATCHING GAME

Freddie has a great game he wants the kids to play—the matching game. The students love this game and it is wonderful for forcing students to focus on the location of the whole note on a flashcard.

I use two sets of **The Thump in the Night, The Secret of Crater Island**, and **The Bass Clef Monster** flashcards. I mix them up and place them down on the floor in rows of equal number. Each student takes a turn turning over two cards that they think will match.

The goal is to see if the class can get all the matches created. What makes this version uniquely educational and valuable for student learning is that the backs of the cards are the black and white staff sides of the cards. They discover that to win, they need to focus on a matching clef sign and location of where the whole note is on the back of the card. When they flip it over and see the illustrated answer, it immediately gives them feedback of whether they read the backside correctly or not. It's a great learning tool they love to play and don't even realize they're learning. Kindergarten through third grade love this game. Just think! Kindergarten students recognizing the placement of notes on the staff!

Lesson 13

INDEPENDENT PRACTICE STUDENT FLASHCARDS

- "Hello, Freddie" Song
- Photocopy reproducible student flashcards, cut and stack
- Plastic Ziploc sandwich bags

PREPARATION

Now that the students are familiar with all three note name books, this is a great time to create student flashcard sets to use in the music classroom and send home with the kids for independent practice. I photocopy these flashcards on colored paper to make it harder to see through the paper to the answers on the other side. If you have hundreds of students as I do, I have the kids help create the flashcard sets.

TEACHER NOTE: There is Digital Access to downloadable reproducible student flashcard sets. See pages 43-46 for more information.

Before the students arrive, photocopy enough for every student. Then cut the stacks with the school's paper cutter and rubber band each stack of the same card together to transport. Lay each stack out around the edge of a table, and remove the rubber band from each stack.

SING "HELLO, FREDDIE"

After students are done singing, give instructions for creating their flashcard set via an assembly line and then a fun activity using them.

- Each student picks up one sheet from each stack, moving in a line around the table.
- At the end of the line, each student picks up a plastic Ziploc sandwich bag and puts their stack of flashcards inside.
- The next student in line becomes their partner.
- As soon as they each have their stack of cards, the partners find a place in the classroom to sit down on the floor, face each other, and quiz each other. It's a good idea to tell them that only one of the partners keeps her or his cards outside of the bag or you may have a confusing mess to pick up at the end.
- When I say "switch," the other partner begins quizzing.
- If time allows, organize the sets of partners in a **double rotating circle**. Tell the students inside the circle that they are "1"; the partner on the outside of the circle is "2." Ask the "1s" to use their flashcard set for quizzing; "2s" keep theirs in the bag.
- When I say "switch," the number "2s" stand up and rotate to the next "1" clockwise in the circle. The new "1" begins quizzing their new partner "2." This allows for great peer coaching/teaching.

The kids love the cards and often keep them to the next year. I can always tell who has practiced and who has not when I do assessments!

Lesson 14

INTERNET GAME REVIEW AND COLORING PAGES
- "Hello, Freddie" Song
- www.FreddieTheFrog.com
- Coloring Pages (see pages 47-52)
- Parent Note

PREPARATION

It is easy to include technology and parent interaction in our music education using www.FreddieTheFrog.com. Because I am a traveling teacher, traveling from building to building and then teaching from a cart in a multipurpose room, I structure my technology days so that every grade level will be using the Internet games on the same day, but at their level. At least twice a year, I use the www.FreddieTheFrog.com website as part of our concept review.

Before coming to class, I download one of the free coloring pages and make photocopies enough for each child. NOTE: PDFs of all the coloring pages are also included via Digital Access that comes with this resource book. On the back of that coloring page, I print a parent newsletter note (see page 42). The parent note describes the value and benefits of music education, what the students are studying in music class, and how they can reinforce basic music concepts with their child at home, including playing the games at the website. It also states when the individual formal assessments are scheduled and how they can help them be prepared. Playing the games on the website will help the students be prepared for the assessment. On internet class day, I wait to hand out the coloring pages with the newsletter on the back until the end of class. This keeps the class focused on the Internet game and not distracted by the coloring sheet.

INTERACTIVE INTERNET DAY

On our Internet Day, we play the games that function as reviews of what we've been studying at their grade level. Click on "Games" from the Home page of www.FreddieTheFrog.com and you're ready to start! I ask one student or the class to dictate where I should move the computer mouse. Of course, if you are using a Promethean board or Smartboard, students can easily take turns playing the games and being the mouse conductor. Close to the end of class, I click on the "COLORING" tab where the coloring pages are located. The kids get very excited about the coloring pages, so I tell them that I chose one to download and they each get one that day. If they prefer a different coloring page, or all of the coloring pages, they can download and print as many as they want at home if they have the Internet access from their computer and their parents' permission. As I finish the lesson, I give each student a coloring page to take home. I point out that the coloring page has the website written on it and quickly describe where to type it into the address bar with their parents' permission. Some kids will share that they don't have the Internet at home, and I assure them that I understand and that's fine. I point out other places that they can go to a computer and on the Internet, such as the library, or possibly grandparents' home. Just ask their parents.

Our Interactive Internet Day creates a lot of excitement among the students, and by playing the games as a group at school and handing them a coloring page with the website on it, most of your students will go home and want to play and ask their parents how they can get online. The games at www.FreddieTheFrog.com will only enhance your program and get more parents excited about what their child is learning in music class.

HOW OFTEN DO I SHARE THE FREDDIE BOOKS IN CLASS?

I only share each book once in the beginning of the year and do quick reviews with the flashcard sets for the rest of the year. Half way through the year, I share them each once again, to refresh memories and introduce Freddie to the kids that moved in later in the year and missed out on the stories the first time around.

30   BEYOND THE BOOKS – TEACHER GUIDE

ASSESSMENT TOOLS AND IDEAS

I began assessing many years ago to test my teaching strategies. I quickly discovered that I learned far more about my students and garnered my parents' support!

As music teachers with limited class time, we tend to do most activities in large groups, with little one-on-one interaction. My job entails traveling between five K-3 buildings and teaching 420 students twice a week for 25-minute periods. Informal assessments of the general group are fairly easy, but I like to assess the individual in a one-on-one situation twice a year. So I use a combination of informal group and individual one-on-one assessments. Flashcards create an easy way to assess my students. You may lump all the flashcards together and use in a classroom setting or spend time with each child individually at some point in the year. I also have a checklist handy with formative assessment on the fly.

These one-on-one situations are the only two times I see each child individually, although only for a few minutes. The benefits of seeing each child by themselves outweigh the lost time from group instruction. In our situation as music teachers, we always see our kids as groups. We easily notice the child that is very bright and always raises their hand and seems very engaged, but we overlook the students that are quiet and are soaking in the information like sponges, but not very verbal. Every year and every testing assessment session, I am pleasantly surprised how well some students do because they appeared to not be paying attention, or not understanding. I also am surprised by students who I thought understood based on what I observed in class, but in actuality are having difficulty and missing an important piece of a concept. By simply spending a couple of minutes alone with them, they understand. That's powerful! I also find that the shy students feel more connected to me after the individual assessment. Many look forward to those few moments alone with the teacher.

By working with the child verbally one-on-one, showing them a flashcard and asking them to answer all by themselves, there is no question whether they know it or do not know it because we have been practicing doing this as a group multiple times. So this is the surest assessment with the method that I teach. It also gives me an opportunity to help that student if he or she is struggling with a concept.

FLASHCARDS

I use the following flashcard sets:

- Freddie the Frog® Note Name Flashcards (via Digital Access)
- Tempo flashcards: *andante, allegro, largo, presto* (via Digital Access)
- Dynamics flashcards: *p, mp, mf, f* (via Digital Access)
- Selected rhythm flashcards (#44223117, Cheryl Lavender, Hal Leonard Publishing)
- Selected melody flashcards (# 44223118, Cheryl Lavender, Hal Leonard Publishing)

I prefer not to spend class time having my students complete worksheets for assessment. With kids at the K-3 level, administering a written test will be a barrier to answering the question correctly for many, unless you have **practiced** doing worksheets. When students miss a question, you have no way of knowing whether it was because they did not understand how to do the worksheet or they did not know the answer.

HOW DO I DO THIS?

I manage the class by showing videos during the individual testing. I choose video clips that I feel are not part of the mainstream and that most kids have not seen before. They have a music connection that we can come back to in later classes. For example, a video of *Peter and the Wolf* is one that they watch. Later in the year, we act it out in our class while listening to the classical music and matching the instrument to that character. While the group is watching the video, I pull one student at a time to the side of the room to respond to a set of flashcards. If a child is struggling, I use this time to re-teach a concept.

MUSIC ASSESSMENT REPORT

When individually testing a student, I record responses directly on an assessment report sheet (see pages 35-37) while the student is answering. I include rhythm reading, note recognition, sight-singing, pitch matching, and tempo and dynamic terms. Parents understand these terms enough to realize that their children, at a young age, are learning how to read music, and that makes sense to them. On the backside of the assessment sheet, I include a rubric that shows what is expected at each grade level (see page 38). This gives them something to compare and see the sequential growth. I also post this on the music page of our school district website.

I do not include everything that I assess on the assessment report sheet. If you are checking off your national standards in your music classroom, there are many standards that will not seem as valuable to the parents. For example, the cross-curricular piece or the historical piece will not seem as important to them and they won't understand what it means when mentioned on the report. I make sure that I include things that make sense to parents.

These report sheets are printed on blue paper and designed to fit inside the report card. I quickly write a personal note of praise at the bottom of the report sheet as well. Whatever that student does very well, such as matching pitch, keeping a beat, or just a joy to have in class, I scribble on the bottom. This personal note means a lot to parents.

I keep the assessment sheets until grade card time, and then the classroom teachers insert them inside the envelopes and send them home. I do this assessment twice a year, once in the fall with the first quarter grade card, and once again in the spring with the third-quarter grade card. This corresponds with parent-teacher conferences. By sending the music assessment report home with the classroom grade card, it receives a higher perceived value to the parent. When they open the child's classroom grade card and find the blue sheet music assessment, it tells the parent that we take music education seriously and it is part of their whole grade for the class. If you send it home separately in their school bag, or a different time of the year, it doesn't seem to have as much importance even though we know that it is the same value.

The music assessment report with the personalized note makes a special connection that the parents usually share with their child, which reinforces the parents' support of music education and you, the teacher. It also causes the parent to take special note of their child's accomplishments in music and support their involvement. The feedback is tremendous! I quickly realized it was my greatest form of advocacy.

Parents often comment that they don't remember learning music concepts when they were young. It is a strong, silent statement that we take music seriously and there is a whole lot more going on in music than playing games, dancing and singing. Many parents comment on those personalized notes and scores. A few parents have contacted me and asked what they could do at home to help their child excel in music. This system works very well for me and definitely seems worth my time investment.

ASSESSMENT TOOLS READY TO USE

Examples of what I use are included in the Assessment appendix on pages 35-42 and via Digital Access.

ASSESSMENT REPORT SHEET FILES

Pages 35-37 show the student assessment report sheets I use that are sent home to parents. There are sample reports and the actual report sheet ready to print out and use. There is also Digital Access to a PowerPoint file of the report sheets, so you can assess right on your computer, or print out the PDF files that are also included. I have designed a report specifically for Grades K-2, and one for Grades 3-6. I always use blue paper to print the assessment report cards. Using a color helps the reports stand out on their own. It helps the parents recognize that this is something different and it doesn't get confused with all the white sheets of paper and the typical white classroom report card or sheet. My parents are trained to see the blue sheet and know that it represents the music assessment.

GRADE LEVEL EXPECTATIONS

Page 38 is a reproducible sample of what I print out on the backside of the assessment sheet and send home so parents know what is expected at each grade level. A PDF file of this information is also available via Digital Access.

ASSESSMENT SPREADSHEET FILES

On pages 39-41 there are samples of the assessment spreadsheets I use throughout the school year to track my students' progress. There is Digital Access to these spreadsheets as PDFs and as Excel files, so you can adapt them to fit your purposes. Once you've added the students' names in left column, you are ready to assess. I travel with a laptop and record scores while assessing for individual reports. This makes it easy to enter formulas to calculate growth of learning and retention per student. You can also print the PDF forms and pencil in the scores on paper.

INTERACTIVE ONLINE GAMES AND COLORING PAGES

FREDDIETHEFROG.COM

CLICK ON GAMES.

There are **Matching Games** for each note name book and combinations of the books. To play a game with the entire treble clef, click on the treble clef poster image. For all of the note names, click on the Treble Clef poster and the Bass Clef poster image. Each matching game will rearrange the location of the cards at the completion of each round of the game. See how quickly you can solve all the matches. Try to beat your time!

Tempo Island Rhythm Game is located below the image of *The Mysterious Wahoooo* book. It functions the same as the magnetic rhythm board.

1. Create a four-count rhythm pattern by clicking and dragging rhythm notation on top of one of the four counts.
2. Choose and click on one of the tempo terms.
3. Click PLAY to hear the tempo track. After two measures, you will hear your rhythm pattern played by claves. If you prefer not to hear the claves, slide the maraca volume control to the far left. If you need it louder, slide it to the far right.
4. Click STOP to change tempo tracks.

CLICK ON COLORING.

Downloadable coloring pages for each book are also available at the website. Click on the word COLORING, and then click on the coloring page underneath one of the books. The single coloring page will open up to various coloring pages that go with the chosen book.

NOTE: These coloring pages are also available via Digital Access.

INTERACTIVE WHITEBOARD CLIPART

FEATURED VIA DIGITAL ACCESS

If you use the Smart Board, Promethean board, or any other type of interactive whiteboard, you will enjoy using Freddie the Frog® and stick rhythm clipart that is included via Digital Access that comes with this resource book. Just add it to your resource browser library and have fun getting creative!

After you have imported the clipart into your resource library, rename the files with the word Freddie included. When you are doing a search within the resource library/browser, just search for Freddie and all the clipart files will pop up.

INTERACTIVE WHITEBOARD LESSONS

FEATURED VIA DIGITAL ACCESS

I have also included PDFs of three interactive whiteboard flipcharts:

- Freddie's Mystery Song – The Closet Key (see Lesson 9)
- 4-Beat to 12-Bar Fun (see Lesson 6)
- Freddie's Mystery Song – Engine, Engine

There are several versions of the "Engine, Engine" melody and game. Change it to what works best for you and your lesson. I use the following game in my classroom:

Engine, Engine Singing Game

1. Divide the class into groups of five or six.
2. Choose one person to be the first "train conductor."
3. All students sit on their knees in the circle with both hands formed in vertical fists in front of them.
4. The conductor taps each person's fists with his or her double vertical fists with the beat of the song.
5. Whoever is tapped on the last word, "back," is the next conductor. The person that just finished, puts his or her fists behind their back to indicate they are finished with their turn.
6. A fun addition to this game is adding a rotation. Instruct the students that whoever is "out" on the word "back," gets up and rotates to the next circle group and becomes their conductor.

APPENDIX A: REPRODUCIBLE ASSESSMENT TOOLS

Name _Suzy Doe_ Class _2nd - Smith_

Music Assessment
_1st_ Quarter
____ - ____ School Year

5=Mastered (Understands the concept.)
4=Almost Mastered (Understands the concept with minimal help.)
3=Understands (Understands the concept but dependent on help.)
2=Grasps (Recognizes the concept but lacks understanding.)
1=Difficult (Does not recognize the concept.)

Assessment of Music Skills

Note Names:
Identify letter names on the treble clef _5/4_ bass clef _5/4_

Rhythm:
Reading/Speaking/Clapping/Counting
the following rhythms: ♩ ♫ ♩. 𝅗𝅥 𝅘𝅥𝅰 𝅝 ♩ 𝄻 _5/4_

Steady Beat: Keeping a steady beat _3/3_

Music Vocabulary:
Identify dynamics: *p, mp, mf, f* _4/4_
Identify tempo: *andante, allegro, largo, presto fine*

Melody:
Recognizing/identifying intervals of pitches (m,s) _4/4_
Matching pitches accurately with voice _5_

****

_1st_ **Quarter Grade**
Suzy has a pretty singing voice!
She understands rhythm well.

Name _John Doe_ Class _2nd - Smith_

Music Assessment
_1st_ Quarter
____ - ____ School Year

5=Mastered (Understands the concept.)
4=Almost Mastered (Understands the concept with minimal help.)
3=Understands (Understands the concept but dependent on help.)
2=Grasps (Recognizes the concept but lacks understanding.)
1=Difficult (Does not recognize the concept.)

Assessment of Music Skills

Note Names:
Identify letter names on the treble clef _4/4_ bass clef _5/5_

Rhythm:
Reading/Speaking/Clapping/Counting
the following rhythms: ♩ ♫ ♩. 𝅗𝅥 𝅘𝅥𝅰 𝅝 ♩ 𝄻 _3/4_

Steady Beat: Keeping a steady beat

Music Vocabulary:
Identify dynamics: *p, mp, mf, f* _5/4_
Identify tempo: *andante, allegro, largo, presto fine*

Melody:
Recognizing/identifying intervals of pitches (m,s)
Matching pitches accurately with voice _5_

****

_1st_ **Quarter Grade**
John understands rhythm
patterns well. Nice sense of beat!

The original purchaser of this book has permission to reproduce this page for educational use in one school only. Any other use is strictly prohibited.

COPYRIGHT © 2011 BY HAL LEONARD CORPORATION

BEYOND THE BOOKS – TEACHER GUIDE

Name_____ Class_____

Music Assessment

_____ Quarter
____-____ School Year

5=Mastered (Understands the concept.)
4=Almost Mastered (Understands the concept with minimal help.)
3=Understands (Understands the concept but dependent on help.)
2=Grasps (Recognizes the concept but lacks understanding.)
1=Difficult (Does not recognize the concept.)

Assessment of Music Skills

Note Names:
Identify letter names on the   treble clef _____   bass clef _____
clefs by story character names.

Rhythm:
Reading/Speaking/Clapping/Counting
the following rhythms : _____

Steady Beat: Keeping a steady beat _____

Music Vocabulary:
Identify dynamics: *p, mp, mf, f* _____
Identify tempo: *andante, allegro, largo, presto* _____
fine

Melody:
Recognizing/identifying intervals of pitches (m,s) _____
Matching pitches accurately with voice _____
****

_____ Quarter Grade

Name_____ Class_____

Music Assessment

_____ Quarter
____-____ School Year

5=Mastered (Understands the concept.)
4=Almost Mastered (Understands the concept with minimal help.)
3=Understands (Understands the concept but dependent on help.)
2=Grasps (Recognizes the concept but lacks understanding.)
1=Difficult (Does not recognize the concept.)

Assessment of Music Skills

Note Names:
Identify letter names on the   treble clef _____   bass clef _____
clefs by story character names.

Rhythm:
Reading/Speaking/Clapping/Counting
the following rhythms : _____

Steady Beat: Keeping a steady beat _____

Music Vocabulary:
Identify dynamics: *p, mp, mf, f* _____
Identify tempo: *andante, allegro, largo, presto* _____
fine

Melody:
Recognizing/identifying intervals of pitches (m,s) _____
Matching pitches accurately with voice _____
****

_____ Quarter Grade

The original purchaser of this book has permission to reproduce this page for educational use in one school only. Any other use is strictly prohibited.

COPYRIGHT © 2011 BY HAL LEONARD CORPORATION

Name _____ Class _____

Music Assessment

_____ Quarter
- - -
_____ School Year

5=Mastered (Understands the concept.)
4=Almost Mastered (Understands the concept with minimal help.)
3=Understands (Understands the concept but dependent on help.)
2=Grasps (Recognizes the concept but lacks understanding.)
1=Difficult (Does not recognize the concept.)

Assessment of Music Skills

Note Names:
Identify letter names on the   treble clef _____
clefs.   bass clef _____

Rhythm:
Counting the following rhythms : _____

Steady Beat: Keeping a steady beat _____

Music Vocabulary:
Identify dynamics: *pp, p, mp, mf, f, ff* _____
Identify tempo: *andante, allegro, largo, presto*
fine, accelerando, ritardando _____

Melody:
Recognizing/identifying intervals of pitches (m,s, l) _____
Matching pitches accurately with voice _____
****

_____ Quarter Grade

Name _____ Class _____

Music Assessment

_____ Quarter
- - -
_____ School Year

5=Mastered (Understands the concept.)
4=Almost Mastered (Understands the concept with minimal help.)
3=Understands (Understands the concept but dependent on help.)
2=Grasps (Recognizes the concept but lacks understanding.)
1=Difficult (Does not recognize the concept.)

Assessment of Music Skills

Note Names:
Identify letter names on the   treble clef _____
clefs.   bass clef _____

Rhythm:
Counting the following rhythms : _____

Steady Beat: Keeping a steady beat _____

Music Vocabulary:
Identify dynamics: *pp, p, mp, mf, f, ff* _____
Identify tempo: *andante, allegro, largo, presto*
fine, accelerando, ritardando _____

Melody:
Recognizing/identifying intervals of pitches (m,s, l) _____
Matching pitches accurately with voice _____
****

_____ Quarter Grade

OK TO REPRODUCE

The original purchaser of this book has permission to reproduce this page for educational use in one school only. Any other use is strictly prohibited.

COPYRIGHT © 2011 BY HAL LEONARD CORPORATION

BEYOND THE BOOKS – TEACHER GUIDE   37

Understanding Music Assessment

It is really exciting to watch the students develop their musical skills. The students are tested individually in October and April to chart their musical growth and understanding. The assessment sheet reflects the individual assessment.

Similar to a spoken language, the learning of the language of music is sequential. The elements of music are introduced through Freddie the Frog music stories, singing, playing instruments, activities, and games. Each year, music concepts are re-introduced, reviewed and taught at a higher level. We have developed a guideline of expectations for each grade level.

Music Concepts	Kdg grade	1st grade	2nd grade	3rd grade
Note Names Identify Treble and Bass Clef note names by using:	Story characters from Freddie the Frog books.	First letter of story character names from Freddie the Frog books.	First letter of story character names or by music alphabet order.	Mnemonics, or by first letter of story character names, or by music alphabet.
Rhythm Identify and perform given rhythms:	Chanting using "ta," "ti-ti," or "shh." ♩ ♫ 𝄽	Chanting and tapping ♩ ♫ 𝄻 𝄼 𝄽	Chanting and tapping ♩ ♫ 𝄻 𝄼 𝄽 ♪ ♩.	Counting and tapping with numbers
Steady Beat Identify and walk/tap/play given beat:	Distinguish between beat and rhythm of a 2/4, or 4/4 music.	Distinguish between beat and rhythm of a 2/4, or 4/4 music.	Distinguish between beat and rhythm of a 2/4, 4/4, or 6/8 music.	Distinguish between beat and rhythm of a 2/4, 4/4, 3/4, or 6/8 music.
Expression Identify and demonstrate dynamic and tempo terms:	Dynamics: *p* and *f* Tempos: *andante, allegro, largo, presto, fine*	Dynamics: *p, mp, mf, f* Tempos: *andante, allegro, largo, presto, fine*	Dynamics: *p, mp, mf, f* Tempos: *andante, allegro, fine, largo, presto, accel, rit.*	Dynamics: *pp, p, mf, f, ff* Tempos: *andante, allegro, fine, largo, presto, accel, rit.*
Melody Identify: Sing pitches:	Intervals: So-mi Echo singing	Intervals: So-la-so-mi Echo singing	Intervals: S-l-s-m-do Echo singing	Intervals: S-l-s-m-do Echo singing

The original purchaser of this book has permission to reproduce this page for educational use in one school only. Any other use is strictly prohibited.

COPYRIGHT © 2011 BY HAL LEONARD CORPORATION

TREBLE CLEF ASSESSMENT

Classroom Teacher	TREBLE CLEF Grade - 1st Semester	TREBLE CLEF Grade - 2nd Semester	TREBLE CLEF Note Name Identification	1st Semester	2nd Semester	1st Semester	2nd Semester	1st Semester	2nd Semester	1st Semester	2nd Semester	1st Semester	2nd Semester	1st Semester	2nd Semester	1st Semester	2nd Semester	1st Semester	2nd Semester	1st Semester	2nd Semester	1st Semester	2nd Semester	1st Semester	2nd Semester	1st Semester	2nd Semester

2008 copyright Sharon Burch. Mystic Publishing, Bradley Bank Bldg., 2nd Floor, 307 N 13th, Centerville, IA 52544

OK TO REPRODUCE

The original purchaser of this book has permission to reproduce this page for educational use in one school only. Any other use is strictly prohibited.

COPYRIGHT © 2011 BY HAL LEONARD CORPORATION

BEYOND THE BOOKS – TEACHER GUIDE 39

BASS CLEF and TEMPO ASSESSMENTS

Classroom Teacher																
BASS CLEF Grade - 1st Semester																
BASS CLEF Grade - 2nd Semester																
BASS CLEF Note Name Identification																
G	1st Semester															
G	2nd Semester															
A	1st Semester															
A	2nd Semester															
B	1st Semester															
B	2nd Semester															
C	1st Semester															
C	2nd Semester															
D	1st Semester															
D	2nd Semester															
E	1st Semester															
E	2nd Semester															
F	1st Semester															
F	2nd Semester															
G	1st Semester															
G	2nd Semester															
A	1st Semester															
A	2nd Semester															
Bass Clef	1st Semester															
Bass Clef	2nd Semester															
TEMPO - 1st Semester																
TEMPO - 2nd Semester																
TEMPO Terms Identification Assessed																
Largo - 1st Semester																
Largo - 2nd Semester																
Andante - 1st Semester																
Andante - 2nd Semester																
Allegro - 1st Semester																
Allegro - 2nd Semester																
Presto - 1st Semester																
Presto - 2nd Semester																

OK TO REPRODUCE

The original purchaser of this book has permission to reproduce this page for educational use in one school only. Any other use is strictly prohibited.

COPYRIGHT © 2011 BY HAL LEONARD CORPORATION

2008 copyright Sharon Burch. Mystic Publishing, Bradley Bank Bldg., 2nd Floor, 307 N 13th, Centerville, IA 52544

PITCH, BEAT, RHYTHM, & DYNAMICS Assessments

Classroom Teacher	1st SEMESTER GRADE	2nd SEMESTER GRADE	PITCH MATCHING - 1st Semester	PITCH MATCHING - 2nd Semester	Date PITCH MATCHING Assessed	1st Semester Date	1st Semester Date	2nd Semester Date	2nd Semester Date	STEADY BEAT - 1st Semester	STEADY BEAT - 2nd Semester	Date STEADY BEAT Assessed	1st Semester Date	1st Semester Date	2nd Semester Date	2nd Semester Date	RHYTHM - 1st Semester	RHYTHM - 2nd Semester	Date RHYTHM Accuracy Assessed	1st Semester Date	1st Semester Date	2nd Semester Date	2nd Semester Date	DYNAMICS - 1st Semester	DYNAMICS - 2nd Semester	DYNAMIC Terms Identification Assessed	p=piano - 1st Semester	p=piano - 2nd Semester	mp=mezzopiano - 1st Semester	mp=mezzopiano - 2nd Semester	mf=mezzoforte - 1st Semester	mf=mezzoforte - 2nd Semester	f=forte - 1st Semester	f=forte - 2nd Semester

The original purchaser of this book has permission to reproduce this page for educational use in one school only. Any other use is strictly prohibited.

COPYRIGHT © 2011 BY HAL LEONARD CORPORATION

2008 copyright Sharon Burch. Mystic Publishing, Bradley Bank Bldg., 2nd Floor, 307 N 13th, Centerville, IA 52544

K-3 MUSIC AT HOME

You recently received your child's music assessment sheet with the first semester grade card. You'll notice on the backside of the assessment is a rubric describing the grade level expectations in K-3 music. Music, similar to any other skill, is sequential. We start with the foundational building blocks in Kindergarten and keep building upon those blocks throughout the following years, helping your child to read, play, sing, compose, move and listen to music analytically – having fun while learning. Throughout the process, we are developing a musical ear and critical thinking skills through the elementary study of many types of music. Research shows that actively studying music, like learning how to play an instrument, helps develop the neural connections in the brain.

You can reinforce the fundamental skills of music at home through a variety of ways. I use **Freddie the Frog®** books to introduce basic music concepts. Similar to learning math facts, learning note names involves memory work. The students were given a set of note name flashcards. Studying with your child will help them improve their next assessment. If you have Internet access, you can also practice note name recognition and rhythm pattern writing by playing the games at **www.FreddieTheFrog.com**. You will also find downloadable coloring pages with note names and corresponding characters to the stories.

Have fun!

APPENDIX B: REPRODUCIBLE STUDENT FLASHCARDS

There is Digital Access to 40 reproducible student flashcards, ready to download and print. There are 4 flashcards per page. The front of the card shows the music symbol; the back tells the student what it is. See full-size sample on pages 45-46.

TREBLE CLEF NOTES

Space B
Line C (Crater Island)
Space D (Dolphin Bay)
Line E (Eli's Home or Every)
Space F (Freddie's Vacation Home)
Line G (Geckos or Good)
Space A (Azaleas)
Line B (Beetle Bugs or Boy)
Space C (Crocodile River)
Line D (Damselflies or Does)
Space E (Eli's Vacation Home)
Line F (Freddie's Home or Fine)
Treble Clef Sign

BASS CLEF NOTES

Line G (Gate or Great)
Space A (Apple Trees or All)
Line B (Bees or Big)
Space C (Cocoons or Cows)
Line D (Dragon)
Space E (Elephant or Eat)
Line F (Frog Log or Fear)
Space G (Grass)
Line A (Annie the Ant or Ants)
Bass Clef Sign
Staff

RHYTHM NOTATION

whole note
half note
quarter note
two eighth notes
whole rest
half rest
quarter rest
fermata

VOCABULARY TERMS

forte (loud)
mezzo forte (medium loud)
mezzo piano (medium soft)
piano (soft)
largo (slowly)
andante (walking tempo)
allegro (quickly)
presto (fast)

HOW TO MAKE STUDENT FLASHCARDS

- Photocopy reproducible student flashcards, cut and stack
- Plastic Ziploc sandwich bags

Create student flashcard sets to use in the music classroom and send home with the kids for independent practice. There is Digital Access to downloadable reproducible student flashcard sets. Photocopy these flashcards on colored paper to make it harder to see through the paper to the answers on the other side.

If you have hundreds of students as I do, I have the kids help create the flashcard sets.

1. Photocopy enough for every student.
2. Cut the stacks with the school's paper cutter.
3. Rubber band each stack of the same card together to transport.
4. Lay each stack out around the edge of a table.
5. Remove the rubber band from each stack.
6. In assembly line order, each student picks up one sheet from each stack, moving in a line around the table.
7. At the end of the line, each student picks up a plastic Ziploc sandwich bag and puts their stack of flashcards inside.
8. The next student in line becomes their partner.
9. As soon as they each have their stack of cards, the partners find a place in the classroom to sit down on the floor, face each other, and quiz the other one. It's a good idea to tell them that only one of the partners keeps his or her cards inside of the bag, or they may have a confusing mess to pick up at the end.
10. When I say "switch," the other partner begins quizzing.
11. If time allows, organize the sets of partners in a double rotating circle. Tell the students inside the circle that they are "1"; the partner on the outside of the circle is "2." Ask the "1s" to use their flashcard set for quizzing; "2s" keep theirs in the bag.
12. When you say "switch," the number "2s" stand up and rotate to the next "1" clockwise in the circle. The new "1" begins quizzing their new partner "2." This allows for great peer coaching/teaching.

The kids love the cards and often keep them to the next year. I can always tell who has practiced and who has not when assessing!

PARENT NOTE

See page 42 for a reproducible parent note to send home with students about the flashcards and how parents can help their child reinforce what they have been studying in music class.

WWW.FREDDIETHEFROG.COM

WWW.FREDDIETHEFROG.COM

BEYOND THE BOOKS — TEACHER GUIDE 45

AZALEAS
Treble Clef Space "A"
WWW.FREDDIETHEFROG.COM

FREDDIE'S VACATION HOME
Treble Clef Space "F"
WWW.FREDDIETHEFROG.COM

BEETLE BUGS (or Boy)
Treble Clef Line "B"

GECKOS (or Good)
Treble Clef Line "G"

46   BEYOND THE BOOKS — TEACHER GUIDE

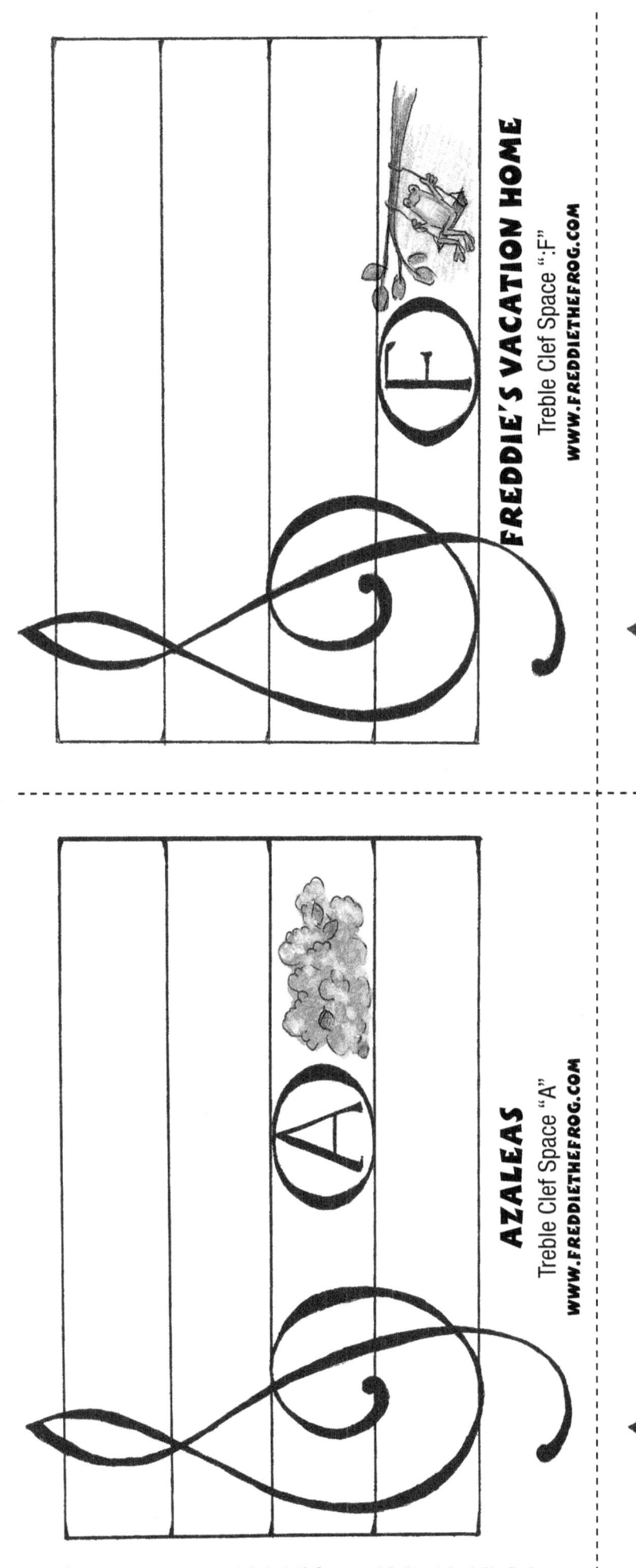

APPENDIX C: REPRODUCIBLE COLORING PAGES
THE THUMP IN THE NIGHT
COLORING PAGES AVAILABLE VIA DIGITAL ACCESS

Download and reproduce these 6 coloring pages to reinforce the treble clef notes learned in Freddie's first adventure.

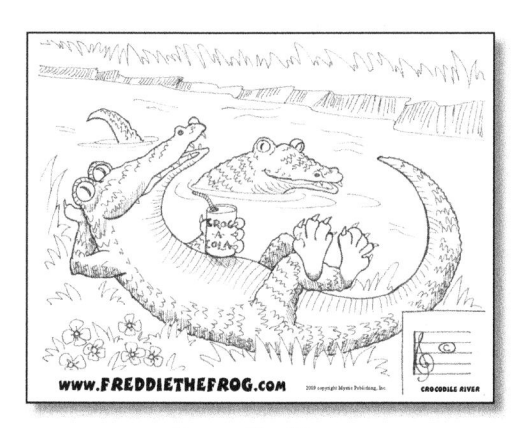

Crocodile River

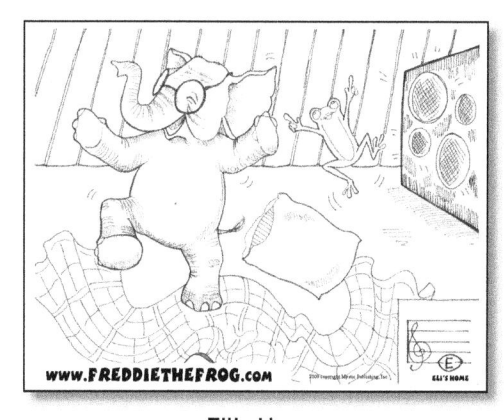

Eli's Home

Eli's Vacation Home

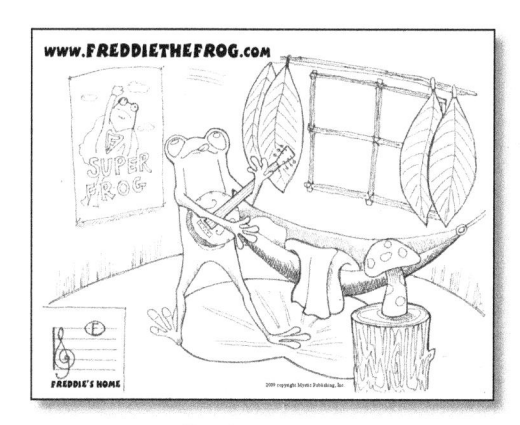

Freddie's Home

Freddie's Vacation Home

Azaleas

BEYOND THE BOOKS – TEACHER GUIDE

THE BASS CLEF MONSTER
COLORING PAGES AVAILABLE VIA DIGITAL ACCESS

Download and reproduce these 9 coloring pages to reinforce the bass clef notes learned in this Freddie adventure story.

Frog Log	Apple Trees	Dragon
Grass	Annie the Ant	Bees
Cocoons	Elephant	Gate

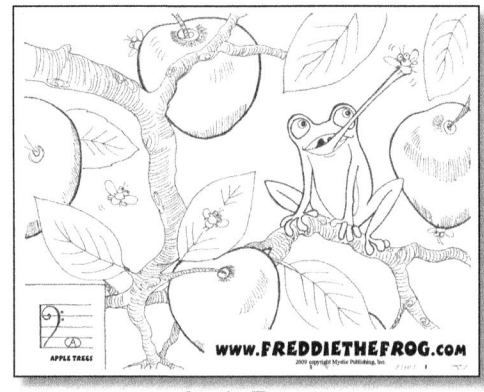

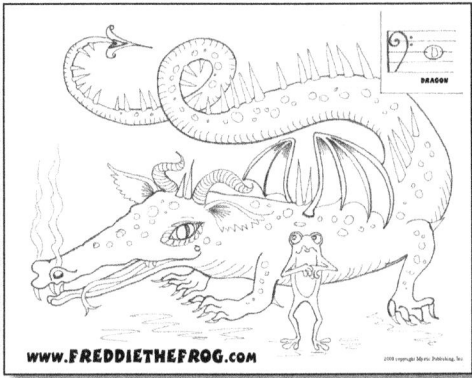

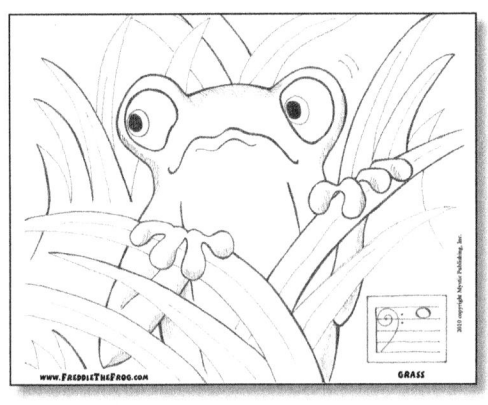

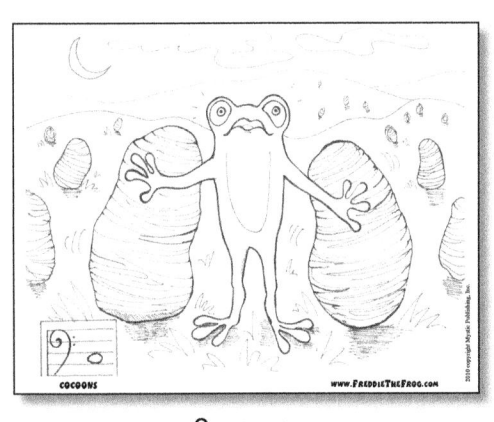

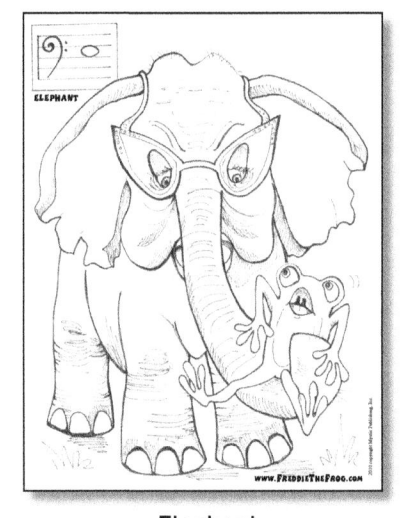

48 BEYOND THE BOOKS — TEACHER GUIDE

THE MYSTERIOUS WAHOOOOO
COLORING PAGES AVAILABLE VIA DIGITAL ACCESS

Download and reproduce these 4 coloring pages to reinforce beat and rhythm learned in this Freddie adventure story.

Bobaloo Baboon

Orangutan-tang

Purple Elephant

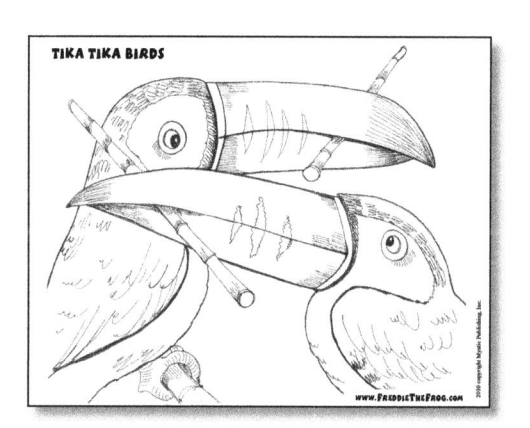

Tika Tika Birds

THE SECRET OF CRATER ISLAND
COLORING PAGES AVAILABLE VIA DIGITAL ACCESS

Download and reproduce these 6 coloring pages to reinforce more treble clef notes learned in this Freddie adventure story.

Beetle Bugs

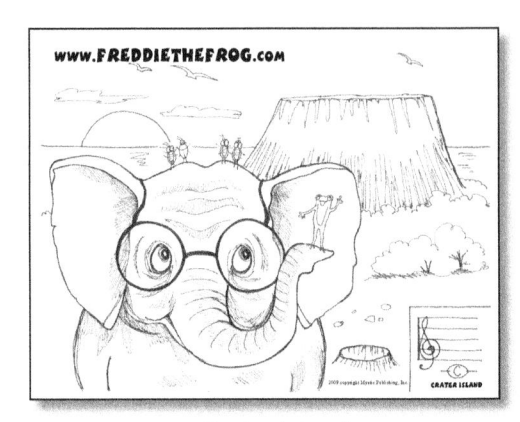

Crater Island

Geckos

Blowhole

Damselflies

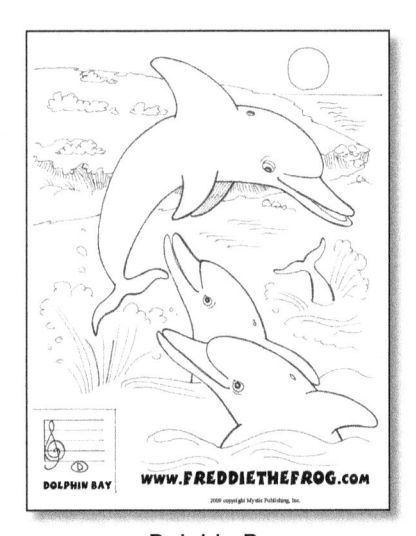

Dolphin Bay

50   BEYOND THE BOOKS – TEACHER GUIDE

www.FREDDIETHEFROG.com

2009 copyright Mystic Publishing, Inc.

BLOWHOLE

BEYOND THE BOOKS – TEACHER GUIDE 51

52 BEYOND THE BOOKS – TEACHER GUIDE

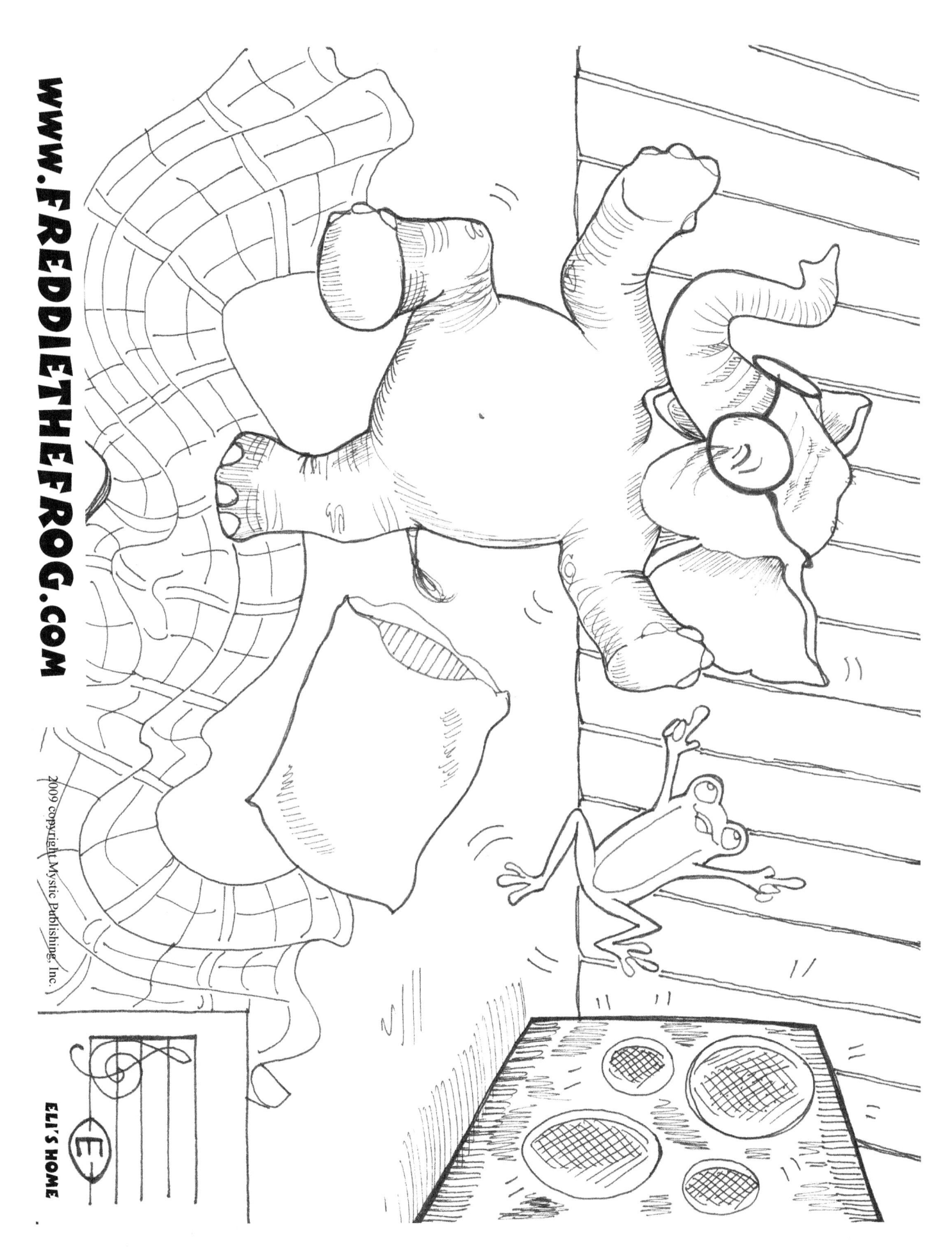

APPENDIX D: WHAT'S AVAILABLE VIA DIGITAL ACCESS?

- **Freddie the Frog® ClipArt**
    1. Stick Rhythms (ta, ti-ti, rest, tika-tika)
    2. Tempo Island Rhythm Background
    3. 5 fun characters: Freddie the Frog, Eli the Elephant, Purple Elephant, Bobaloo Baboon and Orangutan-tang

- **Interactive Whiteboard Lessons**
    1. 4-Beat to 12-Bar Fun
    2. Freddie's Mystery Song – Closet Key
    3. Freddie's Mystery Song--Engine, Engine

The Mystery Song lessons can be used repeatedly by rewriting the rhythmic and melodic patterns with the stick rhythm clipart to create new singing game mystery songs.

You can easily make these interactive by having the students drag dictated rhythms into the boxes to create new songs or solve the mystery themselves.

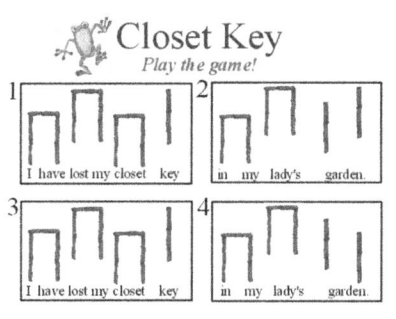

ELEPHANT

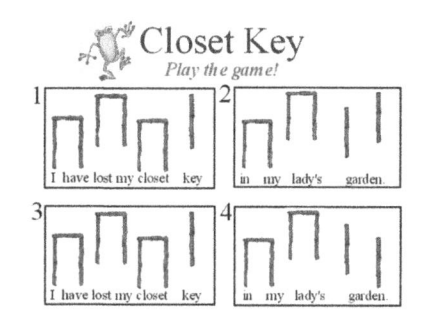

Students can use the stick rhythm images to create an endless amount of rhythm patterns on the whiteboard. You can create rhythm math problems.

TIKA TIKA   **REST**   **TA**   **TI TI**

BOBALOO BABOON

ORANGUTAN-TANG

BEYOND THE BOOKS – TEACHER GUIDE   53

WHAT'S AVAILABLE VIA DIGITAL ACCESS? (CONTINUED)

Start with the Tempo Island Rhythm Background and add stick rhythm notations to create a variety of rhythm patterns.

TEMPO ISLAND RHYTHM BACKGROUND

FREDDIE

- **Reproducible Student Flashcards**
  - Parent Note
  - Treble Clef Notes
  - Bass Clef Notes
  - Rhythmic Notation (Notes, Rest)
  - Dynamic Terms: p, mp, mf, f
  - Tempo Terms: Andante, Allegro, Presto, Largo

- **25 Coloring Pages**
  - 6 Coloring Pages from *Freddie the Frog® and the Thump in the Night*
  - 4 Coloring Pages from *Freddie the Frog® and the Mysterious Wahooooo*
  - 9 Coloring Pages from *Freddie the Frog® and the Bass Clef Monster*
  - 6 Coloring Pages from *Freddie the Frog® and the Secret of Crater Island*

- **Assessment Spreadsheet Teacher File and Student Report Sheet Templates**
  - K-2 Assessment Report Sheet Template in PowerPoint and PDF
  - 3-6 Assessment Report Sheet Templates in PowerPoint and PDF
  - Excel Spreadsheet for the teacher's records to assess pitch, beat, treble clef, bass clef
  - Parent Assessment Information for backside of Report Sheets

NOTE: The assessment files are left in their Excel and PowerPoint form so you can adapt for your purposes. They are also in a PDF form so that they are ready to print and use as is.

HOW TO ACCESS DIGITAL CONTENT

1. To access content in Hal Leonard's MY LIBRARY, go to **www.halleonard.com/mylibrary**.
2. Follow the instructions to set up your own My Library account, so that codes are saved for future access, and you don't have to re-enter them every time.
3. Once you have created your own library account, then enter the 16-digit product code listed on page 1.
4. **Important:** Follow the instructions on the "Read Me First" PDFs for Mac and PC to **properly** download, unzip, open and use these digital files.

KIDS LOVE FREDDIE THE FROG®!

1ST ADVENTURE: TREBLE CLEF

Freddie the Frog® and the Thump in the Night

The first book and accompanying CD narration, introduces the treble clef staff as a map of where Freddie lives. Various lines and spaces represent each part of the story. The staff comes to life through Freddie's adventure and the reader's imagination. The CD includes two sing-along songs as well as author's notes. 10.5" X 8.5" hardcover.

09971507 Retail: $23.95

FREDDIE THE FROG
Teacher's Puppet
09971509 Retail: $19.95

Thump in the Night Flashcards
(set of 6)
09971508 Retail: $6.95

MORE TREBLE CLEF

Freddie the Frog® and the Secret of Crater Island

This book teaches six note names and completes the treble clef staff that the book, *Freddie the Frog® and the Thump in the Night*, introduced. Freddie and Eli discover a buggy world under the azaleas. The two friends join the Blue Beetle Bugs in their quest to find the secret on Crater Island, (middle C)! **Includes** peek-through pages and an enclosed audio CD. The CD includes the dramatized story, sing-along songs, and jam tracks to play along with the 12-Bar Blues. 10.5" X 8.5" hardcover.

09971505 Retail: $23.95

***Treble Clef Island* Poster**

One side – whole notes with letter names;
other side – illustrated answers (as shown above).
09971510 Retail: $6.95

***Secret of Crater Island*
Flashcards** (set of 6)
09971506 Retail: $6.95

BEYOND THE BOOKS – TEACHER GUIDE

BASS CLEF NOTES

Freddie the Frog® and the Bass Clef Monster introduces the bass clef staff and nine bass clef notes. Lines and spaces represent each part of the story. While in hibernation, the staff comes to life through Freddie's dream and the reader's imagination. The CD includes sing-along songs learning Freddie's ABCs (the music alphabet). 10.5" X 8.5" hardcover.

09971501 Retail: $23.95

Bass Clef Monster **Flashcards** (set of 9)
09971502 Retail: $6.95

Bass Clef Island **Poster**
One side – whole notes with letter names; other side – illustrated answers (as shown above).
09971500 Retail: $5.95

RHYTHM, TEMPO, AND BEAT)

Freddie the Frog® and the Mysterious Wahooooo

Discover the tempos, rhythms and beat of Tempo Island with Freddie the Frog® and his best friend, Eli the Elephant. An interactive book perfect for teaching the difference between beat and rhythm, the book guides kids in easily playing rhythm instruments along with Eli and Freddie. The audio CD includes the dramatized story, sing-along songs, and jam tracks to play your own created rhythm. 10.5" X 8.5" hardcover.

09971503 Retail: $23.95

Magnetic Tempo Island Rhythm Board Set
09971504 Retail: $16.95